Celebrations

CW00494264

Festivals in a Multi-Faith Community

Celia Collinson and Campbell Miller

Photographs by David Richardson

John Twinning and Juliette Soester

Edward Arnold

A division of Hodder & Stoughton

LONDON   MELBOURNE   AUCKLAND

© 1985 Celia Collinson and Campbell Miller

First published in Great Britain 1985
Third impression 1989

British Library Cataloguing in Publication Data
Collinson, Celia
 Celebrations: festivals in a multi-faith community.
1. Fasts and feasts
I. Title   II. Miller, Campbell
 291.3′6   BL590
ISBN 0 7131 7441 2

All rights reserved. No part of this publication may be reproduced
or transmitted in any form or by any means, electronically or
mechanically, including photocopying, recording or any
information storage or retrieval system, without either the prior
permission in writing from the publisher or a licence permitting
restricted copying. In the United Kingdom such licences are
issued by the Copyright Licensing Agency: 33–34 Alfred Place,
London WC1E 7DP.

Printed and bound in Great Britain for Edward Arnold, the
educational, academic and medical publishing division of Hodder
and Stoughton Limited, Mill Road, Dunton Green, Sevenoaks,
Kent by The Bath Press, Avon

Preface

In our earlier book, *Milestones*, we emphasised the view that Religious Education is not primarily concerned with passing on to pupils a body of knowledge about religious practices and ideas; it is much more concerned with stimulating thought about questions of meaning, purpose and values, and exploring areas of life and human experience which are the concern of religion in the widest sense of the term.

Milestones explored such areas by looking at ceremonies of birth, commitment, marriage and death. A further area which religions have in common, however, is that all of them celebrate festivals. Indeed, it is human to celebrate! All of mankind appears to have a need to mark special occasions and anniversaries of many kinds by some festivities and ceremonies.

Here, therefore, is another area of great significance which proves fruitful for giving insights into religion and which stimulates thought on what life is all about.

This book, therefore, is an exploration of the major festivals observed within the same five faiths as were explored in *Believers* and *Milestones*. We would emphasise, as we did in these earlier books, that we have set out to portray the festivals as we have found them being practised within religious communities representative of these five faiths in Britain today.

It is our hope that pupils who use this book will come away from their study not merely with knowledge of these festivals, but especially with further insights into the significance of religion and with a greater degree of tolerance for religious views and practices which differ from those they hold themselves.

Acknowledgements

The authors wish to record their gratitude
to the following: members of the various
religious communities for their willingness
to talk to them and help them in their
understanding of the different ways in
which important religious festivals are
observed. They are especially grateful to
those who were prepared to allow
photographs to be taken of these festivals;
Mrs Ivy Gutridge, Secretary of
Wolverhampton Inter-Faith Group, for
advice and assistance with contacts within
the various faith communities; David
Richardson, John Twinning and Juliette
Soester for their willingness to provide the
photographs which form an important part
of this book.

The publishers would also like to thank
the photographers for providing the
photographs as follows:
David Richardson: pp 9, 10, 11, 13, 15t &
b, 16, 19, 20, 21, 25t & b, 26, 27, 31, 32,
33, 36, 371, 42, 44t & b, 45, 47, 48, 49, 52,
57, 58t, 59, 61, 65, 67, 69, 71, 72, 74, 75,
81, 85, 86, 87, 90, 91, 93, 94, 95, 96, 97,
99, 101, 103, 104, 105, 108, 109, 110, 111,
112, 114, 118, 123, 125 & 126;
Juliette Soester: pp 37r, 38 & 40;
Campbell Miller: pp 51 & 58b;
John Twinning: pp 76, 77, 78t & b & 79;
the poster on page 120 was supplied by
David Richardson.

The photographs were taken during the
actual ceremonies and out of respect for
the communities' feelings no flash was
used.

Contents

Preface 3

Acknowledgements 4

Introduction 6

Hindu Festivals

    Introduction – The Hindu
Calendar 7

    The Birthday of Lord Rama 8

    The Birthday of Lord Krishna 12

    Holi 17

    Navaratri and Dussera 23

    Divali 29

Jewish Festivals

    Introduction – The Jewish
Calendar 34

    Rosh Hashanah and
Yom Kippur 35

    Sukkot and Simcha Torah 43

    Chanukah 50

    Passover 55

Christian Festivals

    Introduction – The Christian
Calendar 63

    Christmas 64

    Easter 71

    Whitsun 81

Muslim Festivals

    Introduction – The Muslim
Calendar 84

    The Birthday of the Prophet 85

    Ramadan and Eid ul-Fitr 89

    Hijrah 98

    Eid ul-Adha 101

Sikh Festivals

    Introduction – The Sikh
Calendar 106

    Baisakhi 107

    Divali 115

    Gurpurbs 119

General Tasks 127

Index 128

Introduction

There is something about all mankind which makes us want to celebrate! All over the world, we can find special occasions of many kinds being celebrated in a variety of ways. Indeed, it appears that we almost look for excuses to celebrate! What, after all, is special about a 25th wedding anniversary that is not special about a 24th or a 26th!

Since celebrations are common to all mankind, it is not surprising that they play an important part in religion. So we find that in all the major world faiths there are many festivals celebrated annually, in which some significant aspect of belief or practice within that faith is remembered and emphasised.

This book sets out to help you explore the more important of such festivals which are observed within the five major religions practised in Britain today – Hinduism, Judaism, Christianity, Islam and Sikhism.

In almost every case, a religious festival has a festival story behind it, so you will find in each chapter such a story, followed by an exploration of the way we have found the festival being celebrated by those who belong to that faith within our community.

In following the course offered by this book, you will learn facts about the various faiths and their festivals. It is our hope, however, that you will also take the opportunity afforded by this study to think more deeply about why such festivals are celebrated, why the events and beliefs lying behind them are so significant, and that this will help you in your own personal search for meaning and purpose in life.

Hindu Festivals
Introduction

Hinduism, the religion of India, has many festivals, some of which are universally celebrated by Hindus, others which are much more local to different areas of the vast Indian continent. The Hindu festivals which are explored in this book are some of the best-known and most important ones which we have found being celebrated by Hindus in our own community which is a typical multi-faith community in England.

Some of the practices we observed may not be part of the festival as it is celebrated in India, although the origins of each festival go far back into the roots of Hinduism.

The stories associated with Hindu festivals are found mainly in the **Puranas**, ancient books full of legends and mythological stories. These tales aim at helping ordinary people to understand the very difficult concepts of **sanatan dharma**, i.e. the eternal religion, which is more commonly called Hinduism today. In this section, you will find stories of many gods but it is important to remember that Hindus believe in one supreme being or spirit who is present in everything in the universe; so God – **Aum** or **Om** – can be worshipped in any form, although the Hindu scriptures give guidance about how best to begin finding God in the worship of **avatars**, i.e. appearances of God on earth. In Hinduism, therefore, there are many names for God to emphasise his presence in everything. Pictures and statues are used in worship as symbols which help the worshipper to meditate and remind them of God's many qualities.

The Hindu Calendar

Festivals in Hinduism do not occur on the same date each year as far as the Western calendar is concerned. This is because the Hindu calendar is based on phases of the moon and not on the time it takes for the earth to go round the sun.

There are twelve months in the Hindu calendar, each one having 30 days; this means that a year consists of 360 days. Since that is shorter than the Western calendar, it would clearly mean that a spring festival would sometimes come at a different season of the year! To correct this, an additional month called 'Adhik' is added every few years.

Hindu Month	Western Calendar
Chiatra	April
Vaishakh	May
Jayshyth	June
Ashadh	July
Shravan	August
Bhadrap'd	September
Asvin	October
Kartik	November
Margashersh	December
Paush	January
Magh	February
Phalguna	March

The Birthday of Lord Rama

Hindus believe that when mankind is in great trouble, God comes to earth to help. Such an appearance of God on earth is known as an 'avatar'. According to the **Ramayana**, a Hindu holy book, that aspect of God which is love (Vishnu) came in the form of Lord Rama at a time when the earth was in the grip of evil. According to the story in the Ramayana, Rama was born at noon on the ninth day of the month of Chiatra. This Indian month falls in March or April in England and many Hindus in our community celebrate Lord Rama's birthday at this time.

The Festival Story

Ravana, the king of demons, was causing great trouble in the world and no one could stop him. He had tricked Brahma, the Creator, into granting him a favour. This favour was that no god, demon or spirit would be able to kill him; only a man would have this power. Ravana lived on the island of Sri Lanka and from there he sent his demons out to terrorise the earth and the heavens.

The god, Vishnu, on learning of the troubled state of earth and heaven, resolved to be born as a man.

Meanwhile, on earth, a king was sacrificing to the gods in the hope that his three wives would bear children. This king ruled over Koshala, a northern part of India, and lived in the capital city, Ayodhya. His kingdom was peaceful and

Rama

prosperous for he was a wise ruler and the people were happy. The king, however, had one regret, he had no sons to succeed him. He consulted the priests and asked them to perform a sacrifice to the gods, according to the sacred traditions of the **Vedas**, the holy books, in the hope that a son would be granted to him.

Everything was conducted with great style and the whole city was decorated with garlands of flowers. All of the neighbouring kings were invited to Ayodhya and they came with their priests and warriors. Gifts of food, jewels and gold were given to everyone and there was music and dancing. A special piece of land was selected for the sacrifice which was to go on for a number of days.

The priests lit the sacred fire and directed the worship. On the last day of the sacrifice a figure appeared from the sacred fire bearing a golden dish. Words were spoken to the king telling him that the food in the golden dish had been prepared by the gods and he was to give this holy food to his wives.

The king was overjoyed at the results of the sacrifice and did as he had been commanded. He gave half of the contents of the dish to his first wife and divided the remainder between his other two queens. In the spring, four sons in all were born to the king. The first born he named Rama who became the delight of his parents and of the world.

The second was named Bharata, and the two sons of his third wife were named Lakshmana and Shatrughna.

The four boys grew up together and were trained in the arts of hunting, fighting and riding. Rama, especially, was to need these skills when he grew up, for his role on earth was to fight evil in the form of the demon-king, Ravana, and his demon-followers.

You will learn more of the exploits of Rama on pages 23-5 and 29-30.

The Celebrations

During the month of Chiatra, part of the Ramayana is chanted daily in the Hindu temple. In the photograph on page 10 you can see an open copy of the Ramayana. The book is divided into thirty sections, one of which is chanted each evening. Each section is sung, accompanied by musicians; one section takes about one and a half hours to complete.

On the 21st April, worshippers arrived at the temple between 11 a.m. and 11.30 a.m. and took their place on the carpeted floor. Hymns or **bhajans** were sung to Lord Rama and the singing continued until 12 noon, the time of the birth.

Singing bhajans

The shrine

The highlight of the celebration was the unveiling of the shrine to Rama which had been specially erected for the occasion. This shrine was, in fact, a small cradle which contained a picture of Lord Rama as a baby. Many of the women came forward to rock the cradle as the singing and chanting continued.

The act of worship ended with arti. **Arti** is an act of worship with light and shows devotion to God. The arti tray has five **divas** or candles burning on it. It also holds incense and flowers. These items represent the five elements from which everything else is made: fire, air, water, earth and gases. The tray is moved continually in front of the shrine while the arti hymn is sung.

On this occasion, those worshippers nearest to the shrine waved the arti tray in circles in front of the picture of Lord Rama. As the hymn concluded, the arti tray was taken among the worshippers who warmed their hands over the flame and passed them over their foreheads. This action showed symbolically that each one had received God's blessing and power.

Hindu ceremonies always end with the giving out of **prashad**, i.e. food which has been offered to the gods during the worship. On this special occasion the prashad consisted of brown sugar and coriander sweets, together with a mixture of milk and yoghurt. This is only given on the birthdays of Lord Rama and Lord Krishna.

We asked Mr Mehan to explain why he thought it was important to remember the Lord Rama's birth. He told us:

'The story of Lord Rama which we recite throughout this month is a model of how a human being should behave and we believe we can learn from his example. Like Rama, we should always oppose evil and should do our duty to the best of our ability, in whatever role we have in this life. Through our worship, we can show devotion to God and gratitude for his love.

To chant the name of Rama or to listen to tales of the god will bring blessings to us. So we come together to worship at special times like these to show our devotion and we leave feeling happy and blessed.'

Task 1
Explain the following terms: arti, prashad, the Ramayana, the Vedas.

Task 2
Write a story entitled, 'The Lord Vishnu Enters the World.'

Task 3
Mr Mehan said, 'We come together to worship at special times like these to show our devotion and we leave feeling happy and blessed.' What do you think he meant when he said they feel 'blessed'? Why do you think showing their devotion to God left them feeling happy and blessed?

Arti

The Birthday of Lord Krishna

Krishna is the eighth avatar of Vishnu, and in paintings is usually represented as the blue god, since he is said to have swallowed all the poisonous sins of the earth.

Lord Krishna's birthday is known as **Janamashtami** and it occurs on the eighth day of the Hindu month, Shravan.

The Festival Story

Ugrasena, King of Muthra, was married to a very beautiful woman. A demon fell in love with this wife of the king and, assuming the guise of her husband, had sexual relations with her. As a result of this union, Kansa was born.

It was very difficult for Ugrasena to love this child, for even in his youngest years he was cruel and spiteful. When he became a man, Kansa rebelled against Ugrasena and had the old man put in prison. He seized the throne and began an oppressive reign of terror. The people tried to resist him but they could not fight against the demons, known as 'asuras', who were Kansa's slaves. He destroyed homes, filled his prisons with priests and took away the power of his nobles. Even the river Yamuna gave up the sacred blue colour of her waters and turned purple as a sign of all the blood which had been shed in the kingdom.

The earth could bear no more horror and entreated the gods for help. Brahma passed on this plea to Shiva, who in turn consulted Vishnu. Once again, Vishnu, out of love for mankind, decided to assume human form so that he could fight on the earth against the evil which had appeared in the form of a man.

Kansa had a beautiful sister named Devaki; when she was of marriageable age, he chose her future husband, Vasudeva, a nobleman in the kingdom. The wedding festivities were very successful and Kansa was in such a good mood that he offered to drive away the bridal chariot himself the next day.

As the horses were speeding along, a voice was heard thundering from the heavens, 'Fool! It is the will of God that you shall die at the hands of Devaki's eighth child!' Kansa, in horror, stopped the chariot and reached for his sword intending to cut his sister in pieces. The bridegroom, Vasudeva, implored Kansa to pause and think about this message from the skies. 'Kansa,' he said, 'the river Yamuna is swollen with the blood of women and children you have killed; think before you bring an even greater disaster on yourself! The voice said that one of Devaki's children would be your enemy; save her life and accept instead each child as it is born!'

Kansa lowered his sword, turned the chariot around and headed back to Muthra. He drove immediately to the prison and handed his sister and brother-in-law over to the guards. His instructions were that they should be guarded carefully and that he was to be informed immediately if a child was born.

The years passed and seven children

The young Lord Krishna

were born to the unfortunate couple but all were destroyed by Kansa. As the time drew near for Devaki to give birth to her eighth child, Kansa grew increasingly nervous; he strengthened the guard, consulted the astrologers about the future and each evening he surrounded himself with musicians and dancers to drown his fears. Each night his sleep was disturbed by nightmares which troubled his soul, a part of himself which he was surprised to discover seemed now to exist!

On the eighth night of the month of Shravan, the Lord Vishnu appeared to Devaki and Vasudeva in his original form. His four hands each held a conch shell, a circular missile weapon like a discus, a mace and a lotus flower. His skin was as dark as the evening sky and he was dressed in red and yellow. He spoke to Vasudeva saying, 'Tonight, Devaki will give birth to her son; take him to the wife of Nandha, the herdsman; she too will be delivered of a child this evening. Place your baby next to her and bring her girl child to the prison.'

At midnight, Lord Vishnu came to earth in the form of Krishna, Devaki's eighth-born son. The child was born on straw in the prison. While the guards were fast asleep, the door of the prison swung open and, quickly, Vasudeva took the child, wrapped in a blanket, and headed for Nandha's home.

The great serpent, Shesha, protected the baby from the bad weather and accompanied Vasudeva on his journey. They came to the flooded banks of the river Yamuna whose waters gushed in a raging torrent. On their approach, the waters receded making a pathway for the infant and his father. Eventually, they reached the home of Nandha; Vasudeva found the baby girl and quickly exchanged her for Krishna. The sleeping mother did not even stir and Vasudeva hurried back to the prison carrying the daughter of Nandha, hoping that Kansa would believe that this daughter had been born to Devaki.

Before daybreak, the guards were awakened by the crying of a baby; they rushed to Kansa with the news and he stormed into the cell intending to dash its tiny body against the stone walls; the tiny infant, however, slipped from his grasp and soared high into the sky, calling, 'Fool! I am the Mother Goddess; the child destined to destroy you is alive and safe from harm!'

Kansa took fright and shut himself up away from everyone else to think of ways of finding the child. Meanwhile, at Gokul, the villagers were rejoicing to hear that Nandha's wife, Yasoda, had given birth to a son. They all came to see the child and to give him their blessings. They passed the baby from one person to another then placed him back in his cradle. Nandha and Yasoda, with the approval of the priest, named the child Krishna, meaning 'dark'.

So the Lord Vishnu had entered the world in the form of Krishna. He grew to have many adventures and to fulfil his role by defeating the tyrant King Kansa. There are many stories about his adventures and they are especially retold on the night when his birth is celebrated.

The Celebrations

This night is one of the longest of the year for those Hindus who celebrate the birth of Lord Krishna. He is said to have been born at midnight so most stay up to celebrate the exact moment of his birth and their worship tends to continue until the early hours of the morning.

We asked Mr Chandra, one of the Hindus in our community, to tell us about the celebrations. He told us, 'The Bhagavad-Gita, an important holy book for those who worship Krishna, is recited each day in the month of Shravan. We read this in a Gujarati translation in our mandir (i.e.

14

temple). We ask a visiting priest to read portions of the text daily to those who attend each day for worship.

'The highlight of our celebrations in this month occurs on the eighth day of the month when the mandir is full of people who wish to offer loving devotion to their Lord Krishna. In the mandir we have three shrines, the central one being dedicated to Krishna. On the occasion of this festival of Janamashtami, we erect a temporary shrine in front of this permanent one: the centrepiece is a picture of Krishna as a child, for this aids our worship on his birthday.

'During worship, the bhajans, or sacred songs which we sing, direct our thoughts to the love of Yasoda for her child, Krishna. Our hymns, written by poets from the sixteenth century onwards, are the focus of our worship and our means of expressing, often very vigorously, our love for the Lord Krishna.

'On this night the worshippers offer sweet foods before the garlanded picture of Krishna; a small cradle, covered in decorations, represents the cradle into

Offering sweet foods

The cradle

Arti

which Krishna was placed as a child; many people come forward to rock this cradle gently. After arti, the sweet foods from the shrine are distributed to the congregation as prashad, holy food which has been offered to the gods.

'Our actions on this evening are a way of remembering the words of Krishna, "Always think of me as your son and also as the Most High, thus you will be united with me." We try in this way to have an intimate, loving relationship with God. When I meditate on the love Yasoda had for Krishna, this serves as a means of concentrating my thoughts on the divine god; he becomes more real to me, and I feel closer to him.'

Task 1
Who are the following characters in the festival story: Vishnu, Ugrasena, Brahma, Shiva, Kansa, Devaki, Vasudeva, Nandha, Yasoda?

What do you see as the most important religious lesson of the story?

Task 2
Mr Chandra said that the aim of the celebrations was to feel close to God. In what way do you think the worship achieved this feeling of unity with God? Use the photographs to help you in your answer.

Task 3
Tell the story of Krishna's birth as if you were Vasudeva. Explain particularly why this birth was seen to be so important to the world.

16

Holi

On the day of the full moon in the Hindu month of Phalguna (which falls between February and March in our Western calendar), there is celebrated a festival which is perhaps one of the oldest known. The festival of Holi is a spring celebration when the darkness of the winter months is almost at an end and colour and warmth are beginning to return to the land once again. It is easy to understand the reasons for such a celebration at this time of the year, for everyone has experienced that feeling sometimes called 'spring fever'! It is a feeling that the months ahead are full of hope; now that winter is over, life seems good again and full of possibilities. Such feelings of fun and joy in living, that many experience, are clearly expressed in this Hindu festival of Holi.

The Festival Stories

There are a number of stories which are said to relate to the origin of Holi. This is not surprising when we remember that the festival has been celebrated for many hundreds of years, particularly in a country so vast as India.

Hiranyakashup and Prahlad

One of the stories tells how, long ago, when Hiranyakashup was king of the demons, he and his demon-followers were continually at war with the gods. There came a day when he defeated the gods in a great battle and proclaimed himself supreme god of the whole universe and declared that he alone was to be worshipped.

Soon after this victory, a son was born to him and he called the boy Prahlad. As Prahlad grew up he proved to be very different from his father: his thoughts were continually on God. This greatly annoyed Hiranyakashup who insisted that the boy, like everyone else, must worship him alone. Since Prahlad stubbornly refused to do this, his father sent him to a very strict teacher with firm instructions that the boy must not be allowed to think of God. The teacher found his task impossible, for even when he taught Prahlad the alphabet, he memorised it by reciting the names of the gods! He would chant, 'V for Vishnu, S for Shiva, and K for Krishna!' Prahlad simply refused to forget God.

When Hiranyakashup heard the teacher's report, he decided that his son must be put to death. He enlisted the help of his daughter, Holika, who possessed powers which enabled her to walk through fire unharmed. Hiranyakashup ordered his men to collect wood and build a bonfire. When it was complete, Holika sat on top of it with Prahlad on her knee. Prahlad was unafraid; he had not really paid much attention to what was going on for, as usual, his mind was so much on God.

The fire was lit and, as it flared up, screams were heard to come from it; they were not, however, the screams of Prahlad, but were those of Holika! She had forgotten that she was only safe in fire if she was

17

by herself, so she was destroyed, but Prahlad came from the fire, safe and well. His secret was that he had forgotten himself and had thought only of God. He was protected because of his goodness which was able to overcome all evil.

Krishna Destroys Putana

Another story told at Holi concerns Krishna. On pages12-14 we read of the birth of the Lord Krishna whose life was saved despite the scheming of his wicked uncle, King Kansa. Kansa had been told that a child was born who would kill him; he believed that this child must be found and destroyed so he sent out powerful demons with orders that they should kill all newborn children. One of these demons was Putana who took the guise of a beautiful woman and wandered from village to village looking at the children; in truth she was the vampire nurse whose breasts were full of poison and any child who took her milk would die.

Eventually she arrived at Gokul, the village where Krishna had been taken for safety. She found the house of Nandha, the cowherd whose wife was looking after Krishna. The baby lay sleeping in his cradle, but Putana, with many loving words, lifted him in her arms. She held Lord Krishna to her breast, but he recognised her true nature. As his lips touched her breast, he drew the life from the demon and she sank to the floor; her beauty faded and her true nature was revealed for all to see. The villagers built a funeral pyre and joyfully burned the body of the fiend Putana; Krishna had destroyed the enemy of all children.

Both these stories associated with the festival of Holi emphasise the idea of goodness overcoming evil and that is a belief which lies behind this ancient Hindu festival.

The Celebrations

In India, the celebrations for Holi usually last for three days. In villages and towns, crowds gather in the streets to sing and dance and squirt each other with coloured water or daub each other with paint! The coming of spring is a time for thanksgiving and joy. Most people wear their old clothes and join in the fun, or else they stay safely indoors!

The celebrations by Hindus in England are equally joyful but rather more restrained. The Hindus in our community celebrated Holi for one day only but preparations for the festival began long before the day. Part of the celebration involved a special service in the temple followed by a communal gathering round a huge bonfire. The men and boys had been busy collecting wood to pile on the bonfire which would not be lit until the Holi evening. Special foods had been prepared in the temple for the festivities.

At the Temple

Lalita Minstry, one of the young Hindus in the community, told us how she had been looking forward to Holi for many days, as had all the other Hindu children in the area. The evening of the celebration finally arrived and Lalita and her family set out for the temple just before 6 p.m. The temple was crowded and already there were many small children present for this was their special night. No one seemed to mind the noise or the fidgeting of the little ones; the temple was gaily decorated and there was a strong smell of incense in the air. On the main shrine, Lalita could see the statue of Krishna together with his consort, Radha. The lights were directed on to these figures which, earlier, the priest had carefully washed with scented water. Lalita knew that as the priest washed the figures he would have been chanting songs in the ancient language of Sanskrit about

Krishna and Radha

the holy rivers Janauna and Ganges. The statues had also been clothed after this washing and the priest had decorated them with tinsel. Everyone obviously held them in great honour.

The people, who were all seated on the floor, clapped their hands and sang bhajans in chorus. These bhajans, or hymns, directed their minds to God, as did the other chants which frequently occurred, of 'Hare Krishna, Hare Krishna'. Sometimes this chanting of the name of Lord Krishna lasted for five minutes at a time. As they sang, the worshippers were accompanied by the musicians with a harmonium, a tabla and a tamboora.

19

Arti

The highlight of the worship was arti, or worship with light, in which everyone joined. The worshippers stood to recite the hymn; Lalita joined in the chorus:

'Victory to the Supreme Being, O my Lord, victory to you for rescuing your devotees from worldly trouble and distress.'

As they sang, the arti tray, the large plate holding the divas or candles, was moved first to the shrine, then towards the people. Next came the prayers for forgiveness and finally a prayer in Sanskrit:

'Lord, lead me from the wrong paths to the right, from all wrongs to truth, from darkness to light, from death to immortal life.'

The arti tray was taken around the worshippers and they warmed their hands over the flames then passed them over their foreheads. After this action, Lalita, in common with all the other worshippers, placed a coin on the tray as an offering. Finally, everyone received the prashad, the holy food which had been placed before the gods before the service began. This consisted of almonds, nuts and fruit.

The Bonfire

After this worship in the temple, they all went out into the darkness carrying objects to offer to the fire once it was lit. They made their way to the huge bonfire and awaited the priest who was to light it. Soon the whole scene was lit up by the blaze and the offerings were made to the fire. Parents picked up their small children and walked around the fire a number of times. Lalita's

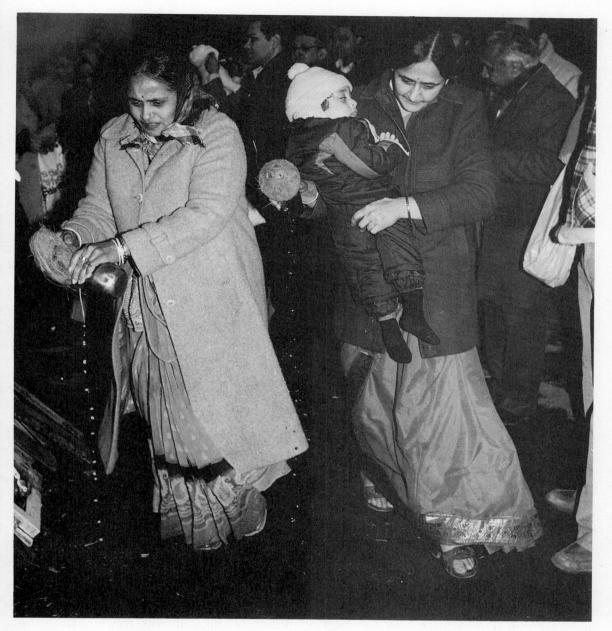

Mothers circle the fire with their children

mother, in common with many others, had already placed a coconut into the fire before it was lit, saying a prayer as she did so. After a time, these coconuts were retrieved from the fire, broken open and eaten as prashad; since they had been offered to the fire, they had now become 'holy food'. Finally, when the fire died down, it was time to leave; for Lalita, and all the other children especially, it had been an exciting occasion which would be long remembered.

An Interview about Holi

We put some questions about this festival to Mr Patel, one of the Hindus in our community.

Our question: From what we have heard about Holi, we were expecting to see people throwing coloured water at each other and indulging in such like pranks! Are such things really part of Holi, and, if so, why did they not happen here?

Answer: In India, people do indeed throw dyes and coloured water, but here in England it is not suitable, for it would create such a mess and would get us a bad name! We celebrate, however, with great joy and the children have fun, but we prefer to put the emphasis, for our children, on offering prayers.

People in India who throw colours are remembering the events in the boyhood of Krishna. It is said that he returned on this day to the village, Gokul, where he was brought up, and people were so happy to be re-united with him that they danced as he played his flute. According to the stories, Krishna was brought up as a cowherd before he became a great prince and the people really felt very close to their god when he was with them and acted as one of them. In their happiness, one of the cowherds, in fun, smeared the gopis, i.e., the milkmaids, with a mixture of yellow tumeric powder and milk; the girls in return took their kum kum, a red powder which ladies use for decoration, and sprinkled it on the men!

Many wonderful tales are told about Krishna's youth. Some say that on the eve of Phalguna, King Kansa sent a demon sheep to destroy Krishna while he and the cowherds were at play. Krishna seized the sheep and dashed it against a tree. As the demon died, its blood splattered the cowherds. This blood is represented by the red coloured water which people throw as they remember the rejoicing of the gopis for Krishna's triumph over evil. You see,

the fun which is often associated with Holi has a great deal to do with feeling close to God and rejoicing at the victory of good over evil.

Our question: Why, in your celebrations, did the people offer coconuts to the fire?

Answer: Coconuts do have a religious significance for us: you will often see a coconut on a shrine in a Hindu temple. The coconut represents the perfect food: it contains milk, protein and carbohydrate, therefore it is the perfect offering. In a way, it is like a man – hard on the outside, but once that man finds the truth inside himself, he has found something perfect. Some say that the three eyes on the coconut shell represent the gods, Shiva, Vishnu and Brahma.

Our question: Why do you regard the bonfire as important?

Answer: We are remembering the burning of the evil Putana and Holika who would harm the children and we are offering prayers for their safety; that is why the mothers circle the fire with their children.

Task 1
In what way is the idea of the triumph of good over evil especially emphasised by the fact that Holi is a spring festival?

Task 2
You are a Hindu living in England: write to a friend in India explaining how you celebrate the festival and make comparison with the way it is observed in India. Include reasons why it is different.

Task 3
What do the following contribute to the religious aspect of the festival of Holi: (a) coloured water, (b) coconuts, (c) the bonfire?

Task 4
Write brief accounts of the two stories told at Holi and explain what religious lessons can be learned from them.

Navaratri and Dussera

The two Hindu festivals of Navaratri and Dussera are often known together as **Durga Puja**. Durga is a name for the Mother Goddess and the word 'puja' means worship, so these festivals are all about worship offered to Durga.

Navaratri lasts for nine nights and is followed the next day by Dussera. All ten days are specially set apart to remember Durga, and Hindu worshippers dedicate themselves to this goddess who is often also known as 'Mataji' or 'Amabaji'. The festival begins on the first night of the Hindu month of Asvin, which in our calendar means that it is celebrated in September or October.

Hindus think of God as having many different qualities and among them are the important qualities associated with being a mother. Just as a young child when it feels threatened by danger will turn to its mother for love and protection, so too human beings turn to God. In this respect, Hindus say that God's love is like that of a mother. This idea is symbolised in the goddess Durga, who is also thought of as the creative force of the universe. When she is depicted it is always with weapons carried in each of her eight hands, in order to defend mankind against evil.

The Festival Story

The festival is celebrated in memory of Rama's appeal to the goddess Durga when he was in great trouble.

Durga

Rama Fights Against Evil

On pages 8-9 you can read of the birth of the Lord Rama. The book which tells of his exploits describes how he grew up to be a fine young man and eventually married a beautiful girl named Sita. Rama's father, the King of Koshala, wished to see his first-born son crowned as his successor before he died, so he summoned Rama and told him his plans. The news spread quickly and the citizens who heard of this forthcoming coronation were happy for they loved Rama and were delighted to have him as their king.

There was, however, one person who was not pleased: this was the serving-maid of Queen Kaikeyi, the second wife of the king. This old and devoted servant was called Manthara and she thought that Bharata, Kaikeyi's son, had just as much right to the throne as Rama. She persuaded her mistress that if Rama was crowned king, his mother would be the most honoured among the queens, while Bharata and Kaikeyi would be little more than slaves. At first Kaikeyi was unwilling to listen, for she too admired Rama, but there is danger in listening to foolish talk, and eventually she was persuaded to believe what the jealous old servant said.

Kaikeyi decided to act on her servant's advice; when the king returned to the palace, he found her in a distressed state and tried to comfort her but, as he listened to her strange request, his blood ran cold. The queen reminded him of a promise he had made to her years ago, when, because she had saved his life, he had said he would grant any two wishes she desired. At the time, she had all that she wanted but now she had two favours which she would like him to grant. The first was that her son, Bharata, should be king; the second was that Rama should be banished from the kingdom for fourteen years. The king was a man of his word and granted her wishes, even though it meant that he died of grief when Rama and his bride, Sita, left the kingdom.

Rama and Sita, together with his brother, Lakshmana, went off to live in the forest. Bharata, who was away visiting relations, returned home to find his father dead and the people grieving at Rama's departure. He was very angry at his mother's scheming and set out to find Rama and persuade him to return. When he approached Rama, however, Rama felt that it was his duty to fulfil his father's promise and he felt he must remain in exile, so Bharata returned to reign in his place. He did not, however, dress as a king and even placed Rama's sandals on the throne to signify that his brother was the true king.

In the forest, Rama, Sita and Lakshmana had many adventures, but one exploit in particular brought great danger to them. Shurpanakha was sister of Ravana, king of the demons: apparently Rama and Lakshmana had insulted her and Ravana decided to avenge the insult.

Accompanied by a demon, Mariach, Ravana in the guise of a priest entered the forest looking for Rama. Mariach changed his form and became a golden deer whose appearance so entranced Sita that she asked Rama to pursue the deer and capture it for her. During the chase, Rama realised that the deer was really a demon so, taking his bow and arrow, he shot the beast. As the demon died, it took its true shape, but imitated Rama's voice, crying, 'Lakshmana, rescue me!'

Lakshmana hurried to Rama's aid and Sita was left alone in their forest dwelling. This was Ravana's chance to obtain his revenge. He came close to the cottage begging for food, but as Sita stepped forward to help him he reverted to his original form, grasped Sita in his arms and took her captive to his island palace in Sri Lanka.

Rama and Lakshmana discovered that Sita had been captured by Ravana and set out on a long search to find her. They enlisted the help of Hanuman, the monkey king, who eventually found Sita on the island. Rama made preparations to fight Ravana; he gathered an army and invaded Sri Lanka. There was a tremendous battle which raged for days and Rama finally prepared to meet Ravana face to face.

The Nine Days of Prayer
Rama prayed to the goddess Durga for seven days, then set out next day to fight his enemy. At the sight of the demon he appealed again to Durga saying, 'All hail O Creator of life who nourishes all

24

Shrine to Durga

broadcast the news that the well-loved Rama was on his way; the rightful king was returning in triumph. When Rama and Sita arrived, therefore, the people were prepared and a tremendous welcome awaited the returning hero.

Celebrating the Festival Today

The Hindus in our community hired a hall large enough for all those who wished to attend the ten nights of celebration. They decorated the hall with streamers, tinsel, pictures of the gods and many bright lights. In the centre they placed a shrine to the goddess Durga.

On the first evening, many worshippers arrived by 6 p.m. to sit around the shrine and sing bhajans. This hymn singing went on for about two hours and was followed by arti, the act of worship involving lights (see page 10). The spirit of Durga is said to be able to enter a person during arti and, indeed, one lady near to us during the worship began to tremble violently; such occurrences are quite likely especially at the celebration of Navaratri.

Singing bhajans

creatures, I salute you!' Rama felt a new surge of power as he fell on the king of demons and slew him. On the following day, Rama offered sacrifices to Durga in her honour and in thanksgiving for his defeat of evil. Rama had, therefore, prayed to Durga for nine days in all, at this most difficult period in his life, and the goddess had given him power to resist and defeat evil.

The Tenth Day
Rama and Sita began their journey back to the kingdom which they had left years before. Hanuman was sent ahead to

A bowl containing grey ash was passed round and everyone dipped a finger in the ash and marked their forehead with it. The ash was in fact from the joss-sticks or incense sticks which had been burning during the earlier part of the ceremony. By marking the forehead, the worshippers were indicating their desire to open their minds to God.

There were musicians assembled on the stage at one end of the hall and, on a signal that the 'garba' should begin, they began to play. The **garba** is a dance; the name comes from a Sanskrit word 'garbha' which means 'the womb'. It is so called because it is in honour of the Mother Goddess. The dance was begun with the older women who have attended many Navaratri ceremonies year after year. They made a circle around the shrine and moved round, clapping their hands in time to the music and chanting the bhajans which were being led from the stage. Soon many other younger women joined in, all of them wearing new saris.

Next the children joined in, the very young being helped by the adults until they were familiar with the movements. After this it was the turn of the men: their dance was vigorous and became faster and faster. Finally there was a dance in which the

The dance begins

The garba

dancers held gaily coloured sticks; two circles of dancers faced each other and moved round quickly with graceful and skilful movements of their sticks. By the end of the evening, feelings were high and some people became very emotional when it was time for the final arti at midnight. The worshippers departed taking with them some prashad (see page 11).

During the nine nights of Navaratri, these festivities and acts of worship were repeated as the people remembered that God will strengthen and protect them if they pray as Rama did when faced with such difficulty.

The Tenth Day – Dussera

The tenth day is known as Dussera and is the day when, it is believed, the spirit of Durga departs from the shrine. On this day the celebrations followed the same pattern as before, but the hall was even more crowded. The dancing stopped at 10.30 p.m. and we all gathered to watch the young people perform a play. The performers depicted Rama and Sita returning victoriously to their kingdom.

Together with Hanuman, they were seated on their thrones and great homage was paid to them. At midnight, the shrine of Durga was dismantled to signify the spirit of the Mother Goddess, thought to have been present throughout the celebrations, departing.

An Interview with a young Hindu

We talked to one young Hindu girl, Pushpa Patel, who had taken part in all the celebrations and asked her about the festival.

Our question: What important lessons have you learned by taking part in this festival?

Answer: Well, I have really relearned many lessons. I think this is why celebrating festivals each year is so important: we are reminded each year of so many important aspects of our faith and way of life. In this festival I have been reminded that evil cannot destroy good qualities if we continue to pray to God. The festival also tells of the importance of human relationships. Sita remained faithful to her husband; Lakshmana was supportive to his brother; Bharata remained loyal all those years to the true king, Rama. We must try to become more like them in our lives.

Our question: What have you enjoyed most about the celebrations?

Answer: I love joining in the dance. In our festivals, music and dance play an important part: these are some of our ways of showing devotion to God. When we join in the dance we feel part of a community and it gives us a chance to express our emotions.

Our question: Why was the shrine dismantled so quickly after the final arti?

Answer: The shrine with the pictures of the goddesses serves as a reminder of some of the qualities of the one God to whom we often refer by the word 'Om'. You will have noticed that when we begin the arti we chant 'Om' three times, for it is this one God to whom we pray. The shrine is therefore dismantled quickly to remind people that these are only images which have helped us to think of God. We do believe, however, that the spirit of Durga has been with us and we have been blessed during our festivities.

Task 1
Describe how Sita, Lakshmana and Bharata remained faithful to the Lord Rama.

Task 2
Imagine Pushpa is writing her diary at the time of this festival: write what you think she might have entered on the evening when Dussera concluded the ten days of rejoicing. Include something about how she felt during the festivities.

Task 3
Do you think dance is a suitable way to express worship to God? Give reasons for your answer.

Task 4
On the final evening of the festival, the young people performed a play telling of Rama and Sita's triumphal return. Write a short play in which you attempt to describe how Rama defeated Ravana and his triumphant return to the kingdom with Sita.

Task 5
Copy the drawing of Durga. Explain what you think is the significance of the weapons she is carrying. (In her right arms she holds drum, shield, cup and water pot; in her left arms trident, sword, snake and bell.)

Divali

The Hindu festival of lights, Divali, takes its name from a shortened form of the ancient Sanskrit word 'deepavali', meaning a row or a cluster of lights. This festival falls in the last two days of the month Asvin and the first two days of Kartik.

Divali is an important festival for Hindus because it marks the beginning of the religious new year. It is a very ancient festival and there are many stories associated with the celebrations. The story remembered in our community at this time, however, is the story of Rama and Sita.

The Festival Story

The story of Rama's defeat of the demon, Ravana, was described on pages 23-5. When this task was completed, Rama was reunited with his wife, Sita. To everyone's amazement, instead of greeting her with joy, Rama was angry and cold towards her and refused to accept her. He said:

'Ravana bore thee through the sky
And fixed on thine his evil eye;
About thy waist his arms he threw,
Close to his breast his captive drew.'

Sita was deeply insulted by these words for, despite Ravana's constant attentions, she had remained faithful to her husband. Such was her distress that she asked Lakshmana to build a funeral pyre.

As the flames grew higher, Sita stepped into the fire but, because she was innocent, the fire did not harm her and she was escorted back to Rama by Agni, the god of fire. Agni said:

'Pure is she in thought and action,
pure and stainless, true and meek:
I, the witness of all actions,
thus my sacred mandate speak.'

Rama gladly accepted his wife since her purity had been proved and he called on those present to witness this:

'Ravana in his rage and folly,
conquered not a faithful wife:
For like ray of sun, unsullied,
is a righteous woman's life.
Be the wide world now a witness,
pure and stainless is my dame:
Rama shall not leave his consort
till he leaves his righteous fame.'

The period of exile was now over and Rama, Sita and Lakshmana now returned to Ayodhya where the people were expecting them. Bharata, who had been governing the kingdom during Rama's exile, made preparations for his brother's return. The whole city was cleaned and decorated, flowers were woven into garlands, flags and banners waved from every turret and tower, and sweet foods were prepared.

Rama and Sita arrived to a tremendous reception:

'Sailing o'er the cloudless ether,
Rama's pushpa chariot came:
And ten thousand jocund voices
shouted Rama's joyous name! . . .
Joy! Joy! In bright Ayodhya gladness
filled the hearts of all.
Joy! Joy! A lofty music sounded
in the royal hall!'

Rama, the rightful king, was crowned with great ceremony. His reign was to prove peaceful and prosperous.

The Celebrations

Preparations

There was no mistaking the fact that Divali was approaching in our community. Notices appeared in the windows of Indian shops selling beautiful material for saris, wishing customers 'A Happy Divali!' The windows of sweet shops were full of delicious foods for this popular festival.

In the homes, mothers and daughters were very busy. Divali marks the beginning of a new year and it is important to begin the new year with a clean house! Special foods had to be made, greetings cards to be written and a trip to buy fireworks was also essential!

At the mandir (i.e. the temple), the preparations had also begun. The children were preparing for the part they would play in the celebrations by rehearsing a dance. The priest had invited special guests to be present for the occasion to speak to the congregation. He had also given the statue of Lakshmi, goddess of wealth and prosperity, a special place of honour on the shrine, for, on the eve of Divali, which is called **Dhan Trausti**, many worshippers come to pay homage to this goddess.

In India, Divali is celebrated for four days, but families in Britain often restrict their celebrations to the eve of Divali and the day of Divali itself.

The Eve of Divali

Worship at the mandir was especially devoted to Lakshmi. The worshippers arrived bringing offerings of food or money, and prayers were offered to the goddess. Lakshmi is the consort of Vishnu and is represented as being devoted to her husband. When Vishnu appeared on earth, Lakshmi accompanied him. He came in the form of Lord Rama and Lakshmi appeared as Sita. On another occasion he came as Lord Krishna and Lakshmi appeared as Radha. Hindu holy books, the Puranas, give clues as to why Lakshmi is worshipped on the eve of this New Year festival:

'From Lakshmi's propitious gaze, men obtain wives, children, dwellings, friends, harvests and wealth. Health, strength, power, victory and happiness are easy of attainment to those upon whom she smiles!'

Lakshmi

Business men bring their accounts

Lakshmi is pictured as sitting or standing on a lotus flower, her symbol, because of her great beauty. Legend says that at Divali she circles the earth, and those homes which she finds clean, bright and welcoming, she enters and brings her blessings.

Shopkeepers and business men brought their account books to the mandir. These were blessed by the priest, and then two shopkeepers, acting on behalf of the whole congregation, performed a special **puja**, i.e. act of worship, to Lakshmi. The priest tied red rakhis (threads) around the wrists of all the men present; these traders vowed to be honest and hard working in the new year and hoped for Lakshmi's blessings. Indeed, all the worshippers hoped for good fortune in the new year as they passed their hands over the flames on the arti tray during the Divali Eve worship.

The Day of Divali

We visited the Patel family to share in their celebrations of Divali day, the day which also marked the beginning of a new year for them.

Mrs Patel woke her daughter, Hemlata, with the words, 'Happy Divali!' Hemlata rose and dressed in the new clothes which her parents had bought her for this special occasion. The Patels have a small shrine in one of their rooms; this shrine consists of pictures and statues of the gods. The family gathered at the shrine and their prayers on this morning were addressed to the goddess Lakshmi. Sweet foods were placed on the shrine and would remain there all day as an offering to the gods. In the evening, this food would be eaten by the family as 'prashad', food blessed by God.

Placing the Divas

Mrs Patel and Hemlata cleaned and dusted yet again to ensure that everything was bright and fresh. As they did so, they placed a diva in each room. Mrs Patel was an expert at making these candles. We were fascinated to see how easy it was to produce

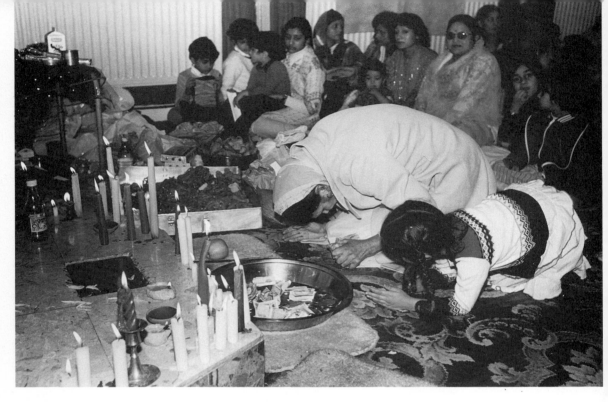

them: she simply kneaded together flour, water and a little oil to make a dough. Taking a small portion of this dough, to which she had added yellow food colouring, she moulded it into a circular shape and made a hole in the middle. She placed a wick of cotton wool, soaked in ghee (melted butter), in the centre of the dough. Each of these divas was placed in a stainless steel dish; it was Hemlata's job to light them later in the day.

Mrs Patel told us that she had made these divas, which are an essential feature of the festival, in the traditional way, but that in many homes ordinary candles are used. Mrs Patel's last job, before settling down to enjoy the New Year's Day, was to sweep the front step. She placed two divas on each side of the step: these were to welcome Lakshmi, but they also served to greet relatives and friends who came to visit. Mrs Patel told us that she often decorated the front step at Divali with patterns to make it look attractive, both for her guests and for Lakshmi.

During the course of the day, many people called at the house bringing cards and presents with them. Mrs Patel offered them the sweet, delicious foods which she had prepared. At lunch time there was a special meal, for at festival time, as is the case in most religions, the sharing of favourite foods is a traditional part of the celebration. Before they ate, Mr Patel thanked God for his blessings and for the gift of life at the beginning of a new year.

Worship at the Mandir
In the evening, the family visited the mandir, their local place of worship, which was crowded for this occasion. Mrs Patel and Hemlata bowed low before the shrine and offered gifts of money before taking their places in the hall. The temple was gaily decorated and many candles were glowing, reminding the worshippers of the central message of the festival – just as light triumphs over darkness, so good will always triumph over evil.

32

As worship progressed, there was no doubting the fact that this was a most joyful festival! Joy was expressed in the hymns which were chanted by the worshippers as they clapped their hands in time to the music; the priest also took up this theme of joy as he related the story of Rama and Sita and their victorious return to their kingdom.

On the day of Divali it is customary to read part of the **Bhagavad-Gita**, a holy book whose title means 'the Song of the Lord'. After the reading from this book, the priest explained the meaning of what he had read. The celebrations in the mandir then ended with the act of worship known as arti; then everyone received prashad.

So the worship ended, and we all stepped out into the darkness which was such a contrast to the warmth and light in the temple. We made our way back to the Patel's home; as we approached, we could see the divas glowing and flickering in every room.

Hemlata had been particularly looking forward to the next part of the Divali celebrations: it was now time to light the fireworks! Everyone had great fun as these were set off and, once again, their bright lights were a reminder of the triumph of light over darkness.

Thoughts on Divali

Before leaving, we asked Mrs Patel if she could briefly summarise what she most enjoyed about Divali. She told us, 'I enjoy seeing my friends and relatives. It is also good to know that on at least one day in the year there is the chance for peace and harmony. This day really marks the victory of light over darkness; it reminds us of the better side of human nature and gives us an opportunity to express love for others. I like to know I can make a fresh start: I can say to myself, "be like Sita every day from now on!"'

Task 1
Use the drawing of the goddess Lakshmi to design the front cover of a Divali greeting card.

Task 2
Describe the preparations made for Divali. Compare them with those made for a festival in any other religion you have studied.

Task 3
What is the essential message of Divali and how is it symbolised in the celebrations? Do you think this is an effective way of portraying the message? Give reasons for your answer.

Task 4
Write the answer which you think Hemlata might have given in answer to the question, 'What do you most enjoy about Divali?'

Reading from the Bhagavad-Gita

Jewish Festivals
Introduction

Judaism is a religion of many festivals. Indeed, out of the twelve months in the Jewish calendar, there are only two which do not have a festival! We have chosen to explore those of their festivals which seem to us to tell most about the Jewish faith and way of life, and which provide the best insights into what this faith considers it is important to celebrate.

Many Jewish festivals probably began as celebrations for some aspect of the agricultural year. As time went on, however, they also became associated with an important event in their history in which they believed God had acted on their behalf. In most cases, therefore, the festival story tells of such an historic event from their past.

The Jewish Calendar

It is obvious that festivals with an agricultural origin will be linked to the seasons of the year. Like those in Hinduism, however, Jewish festivals do not always take place on the same date each year as far as our Western calendar is concerned.

Months

The length of a Jewish *month* is the time it takes the moon to go around the earth: 29 days, 12 hours and 44 minutes. So some months have 30 days and others 29 days.

The Jewish *year*, however, is related to the movement of the earth around the sun!

Twelve moon months adds up to 354 days, whereas a sun year is 365 days. If the Jewish calendar were based purely on phases of the moon, it would mean that festivals linked with a particular season would sometimes fall in the wrong season! To overcome such problems, the calendar was developed to follow a cycle of nineteen years, seven of which are leap years; a leap year in the Jewish calendar means that it has an extra month of thirty days, and this happens every 3rd, 6th, 8th, 11th, 14th, 17th, and 19th year!

The extra month is called Adar Sheni, i.e. 'the second Adar', or simply 'Adar II'.

Jewish Month	Western Calendar
Tishri	September/October
Cheshvan	October/November
Kislev	November/December
Tevet	December/January
Shevat	January/February
Adar	February/March
Nisan	March/April
Iyyar	April/May
Sivan	May/June
Tammuz	June/July
Av	July/August
Elul	August/September

Years

The Jewish year of 5746 began in September 1985; this is because the Jewish calendar, as far as years are concerned, is based on a very old tradition about when the creation of the world took place.

Rosh Hashanah and Yom Kippur

In September or October each year, for Jews there is a period of ten days often referred to as 'the High Holy Days'; some call this period 'the Days of Awe' and others 'the Ten Days of Repentance'.

This ten-day period begins with Rosh Hashanah which means 'the first of the year' and it ends with Yom Kippur which means 'the Day of Atonement'.

Rosh Hashanah is on the first day of the month Tishri, which is the seventh month in the Jewish calendar. It may seem strange to celebrate New Year in the seventh month but Jewish tradition teaches that the world was created on the first day of Tishri and that is why this important festival begins on that day.

Rosh Hashanah – The Festival Story

According to Leviticus, one of the books of the **Torah** (the Jewish scriptures), God instructed the early Hebrew people, the forefathers of the Jews, through their leader, Moses: 'In the seventh month, on the first day of the month, you shall observe a day of solemn rest, a memorial proclaimed with blast of trumpets.' (Leviticus 23 v. 24)

Rosh Hashanah as a New Year festival is essentially a time of new beginnings and, unlike most other festivals, has no festival story as such that points to a historical event which is being celebrated. It is a time when Jews think particularly about their own spiritual life. There are, however, a number of traditional stories about Rosh Hashanah which have arisen at various periods in Jewish history.

There is an old legend which says that on Rosh Hashanah, God seats himself on his throne and the record of all human lives is opened and all the secret thoughts and hidden acts of every person are revealed. Loud blasts on a ram's horn are sounded and a voice announces, 'Behold the Day of Judgement!' Every human being passes before God and he decrees the life and destiny of each one; however, if people sincerely repent of their wrong doing and devote themselves to prayer and performing acts of kindness, they can change the course of their lives and alter the harshness of their fate.

It is interesting to note that the sign of the Zodiac which corresponds to the month Tishri is a set of scales: here is a symbol giving a reminder that, at the time of Rosh Hashanah, there is the idea of one's deeds being weighed and judged by God.

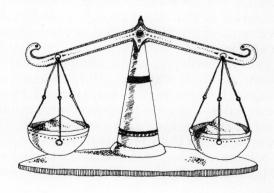

The Celebrations

The month in the Jewish calendar which precedes Tishri is the month of Elul. Elul is regarded by Jews as a time of preparation for Rosh Hashanah. During this month, the **shofar**, referred to in the story above, is blown in the synagogue every day, except on the Sabbath. For the ten days of Rosh Hashanah, the Rabbi wears a white robe in the synagogue and the scrolls of the Torah are also dressed in white covers.

Rosh Hashanah Customs

We talked to the Rabbi and asked him to explain the various customs and ideas associated with this festival.

Our question: We understand that the whole month of Elul is regarded as a preparation for Rosh Hashanah. Can you explain the reason for this?

Answer: Rosh Hashanah is essentially a time of repentance, a time when we show sorrow for our sins and resolve to try to do better. We do not think of that as a sudden, brief turning to God, as if we woke up on the morning of Rosh Hashanah and said: 'I will repent today and tell God how sorry I am for my faults'! By seeing the month of Elul as a time for preparation, we are saying that if one is sincere about repentance and a resolve to do better, one needs time to make the effort and to reflect on the implications of doing this.

Our question: We understand that an important part of Rosh Hashanah and, indeed, the preparation for it, is the sounding of the ram's horn, the shofar, in the synagogue. Will you tell us more about that, please?

Answer: Basically, we think of the loud blasts on the shofar as a call to awake and prepare to leave our evil ways behind. Most Jews will tell you that the most memorable part of the morning service in the synagogue on the first day of Rosh Hashanah is that moment when the notes of the shofar sound out. There are, however,

Sounding the shofar

many other traditions associated with the shofar. Many say that it reminds them of the story from Genesis about Abraham being prepared to offer his son, Isaac, to God as a sacrifice, but God, recognising Abraham's willingness to give his only son, ordered him to sacrifice a ram instead. Indeed, the passage which tells that story is the reading from the Torah for the first day of Rosh Hashanah.

There are some Jews who say that the shofar is blown in order to confuse Satan. On hearing so much noise from the shofar, Satan may believe that the Messiah has arrived and that the end of his power on earth has come!

Our question: Why does the Rabbi wear a white robe at this time and why are the sacred scrolls also dressed with white coverings?

Answer: White is said to represent purity or forgiveness. Since at Rosh Hashanah we are thinking especially about how we can live purer and better lives and we are seeking God's forgiveness for our wrong doing, white is an appropriate colour to remind us of this.

The scrolls

Our question: What about observing the festival away from the synagogue? Are there any special customs observed in the Jewish home at this time?

Answer: Oh yes! We generally have festive meals as a family on both the first and the second nights of Rosh Hashanah. Just as on every Sabbath eve, before we begin our meal, we have a brief ceremony in which we eat a piece of **Hallah bread** and drink some wine, we do the same on these evenings of Rosh Hashanah. The Hallah bread, however, for this festival is round; sometimes it is baked with the shape of a ladder, a bird or a crown on the top. Many say that the ladder symbolises our wish that our prayers may go up and be heard by God; others also link it with the dream

of Jacob from Genesis 28 vv. 10–22, in which he saw a ladder stretching from earth to heaven. The bird symbolises the same idea for many, but there are some who say that it is a symbol of mercy and at this time, especially, we are looking for the mercy of God. The crown is a reminder that we regard God as our ruler and our king. On these occasions also it is customary to have honey on the table and we dip a piece of apple and a piece of Hallah bread into the honey; before eating it we say to each other, 'May it be your will, O God, to give us a good and sweet year.'

Another interesting custom is that known as **Tashlich**, which is a Hebrew word meaning 'to throw away'. Usually on the afternoon of the first day of Rosh Hashanah we gather as a family on the banks of a river or a lake and recite a prayer for forgiveness:

'You will cast all their sins into the depths of the sea, and may you cast all the sins of your people, the House of Israel, into a place where they shall be no more remembered or visited or ever come to mind.'

After this prayer we shake out all the dust and bits of fluff which have gathered in our pockets, or we throw some breadcrumbs into the water to symbolise the idea that we are casting off our sins and making a fresh beginning with the approach of the New Year.

Tashlich

Yom Kippur – The Festival Story

On the tenth day of the month Tishri, there is the day which is really seen as the climax of the important Jewish celebration begun at Rosh Hashanah. It is known as Yom Kippur, the Day of Atonement; atonement means 'to make amends' so this day especially is a day for making amends and for seeking God's forgiveness.

Up until the year 70 CE there was a temple in Jerusalem which was of the greatest importance to Jews. In 70 CE it was destroyed by the Romans. In this temple on Yom Kippur a very solemn ceremony took place. If you study the diagram of the Temple you will see that it was surrounded by several courtyards. The outer one (A), was the Court of the Gentiles; non-Jews were not permitted to go beyond this. Further in was the Court of the Women (B), and next to it the Court of the Men of Israel (C), then the Court of the Priests (D).

Finally, the building itself was divided into two parts – the Holy Place (E) and the Holy of Holies (F). Only priests could enter the Holy Place, but only the High Priest could enter the Holy of Holies and he only once a year – on Yom Kippur. Outside the Holy Place was the altar on which sacrifices were offered. All these parts of the Temple had an important role in the ceremony of Yom Kippur.

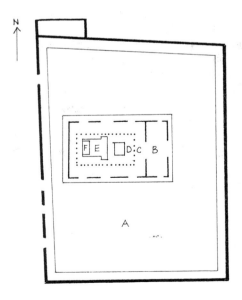

The Ceremony

As the sun was about to set on the evening before Yom Kippur, the High Priest was led to a little room in the Temple. Here he was kept awake all night as parts of the scriptures were read to him and psalms were sung.

Very early on the day itself, many worshippers filled the Temple courts. They were thrilled at the sight of the High Priest in his splendid golden robes offering the daily sacrifice at the altar. After he had done this he disappeared inside the building to emerge later dressed only in a plain, white, linen garment. A young bull was standing near the altar ready for sacrifice. The High Priest laid his hands on the bull's head and recited a prayer.

Also near the altar were standing two goats and beside them an urn containing two gold tablets on one of which was written, 'For the Lord'. The High Priest took the tablets from the urn and, without looking to see which tablet was which, placed one on the head of each goat, calling out so that all could hear, 'A sin offering for the Lord.' The goat with the tablet 'For the Lord' was sacrificed; the other had a red sash tied to its horns and it was known as 'the scapegoat'. Later, as we shall see, there was a ritual in which, symbolically, the sins of the people were loaded on to this goat and it was driven out deep into the wilderness.

In the Holy of Holies

The High Priest left the goats and returned to the bull, reciting the same prayer as before, then he slaughtered the bull, collecting its blood in a basin. He then filled a golden pan with burning coals from the altar and walked slowly into the Holy of Holies where he burned incense and the Temple was filled with its smoke. When he came out, he took the basin of blood, then returned to the Holy of Holies where he sprinkled some of the blood before returning to the altar. Here he slaughtered the goat on which had been placed the tablet 'For the Lord'.

For a third time he slowly entered the Holy of Holies to sprinkle some of the goat's blood. The idea of sprinkling the blood seems to have been that it was thought of as the life of the animal and life is the most sacred and special gift which can be given to God.

The Scapegoat

The High Priest now gave his attention to the other goat with the red sash tied to its horns. He laid his hands on it and recited for a third time the prayer of confession, on behalf of all the people. As he came to the end of the prayer, he turned and faced the people, calling out to them, 'Ye shall be clean.' They responded by calling out, 'Blessed be the Name, the glory of his kingdom for ever and ever.' A priest led the goat through the courtyards and out of the Temple area where another priest waited. The people shouted, 'Hurry and go, hurry and go!' The priest led the goat to a place about ten miles away on the edge of a cliff overhanging a deep ravine. Here the goat was pushed over the cliff and news was quickly sent back to the High Priest that the scapegoat was in the wilderness. In the meantime, he had offered the bull and the other goat as a sacrifice to God, by burning them on the altar.

So all this long ceremony helped the people to feel that their sins had been taken away and God had forgiven them and was prepared to give them a fresh start.

The Celebrations Today

Yom Kippur Eve at Home

On the afternoon of 5th October 1984, the Goldberg family sat down together to eat a hearty meal. It was a happy and festive occasion for this was the eve of Yom Kippur. Although Yom Kippur is a very serious festival, it is not regarded as a time to be miserable!

Mr Goldberg explained to us that they must complete the meal before sunset for then Yom Kippur has begun and they will all fast until sunset next day.

'We are not fasting to punish our bodies,' he explained, 'but we are thinking of the importance of this day which we regard as the holiest in all the year. Some Jews say that on Yom Kippur they are so close to God that they easily forget about their bodies; others express it differently by saying that by forgetting the body they can concentrate all the more on thinking about God and what he wants from us.'

After the meal, the Goldbergs prepared to leave for the synagogue; before leaving, the father blessed the children, placing his hands on their heads and saying,

'May God make you as Ephraim and Manasseh. May it be the will of our Father in Heaven to plant in your heart, love of him. May you wish to study the Torah and its commandments. May your lips speak the truth and your hands do good deeds. May you be inscribed for a long and happy life.'

Other actions performed before leaving for the synagogue were that the dinner table was covered with a white cloth and some Jewish books were placed on it. This was to symbolise the idea that Yom Kippur was being celebrated by fasting, prayer and serious thought. Also a yahrzeit candle was lit as a memorial to dead relatives just as it would have been on the anniversary of a death. (See our other book in this series, *Milestones*, pages 107-12, for information about death in Judaism.)

At the Synagogue

The service began with a ceremony in which the Ark was opened and the scrolls of the Torah were taken out. As on Rosh Hashanah, the Rabbi was dressed in white and the scrolls were also dressed with white coverings. The Goldbergs told us that this service is often called **Kol Nidre** because that is the Hebrew name given to an important prayer which is chanted in this service.

'The words of the prayer,' they said, 'state that all the vows we have made during the past year, but not carried out, are cancelled.'

'Does that mean,' we asked, 'that if you have made a promise to someone and not fulfilled it, you now don't feel under any obligation to do so?'

'Oh no!' they replied, 'the spirit of Kol Nidre is really that we are asking God to forgive us for breaking any religious vows we have made, because this is a time to make a fresh beginning.'

The Goldbergs also said that the rather sad, haunting melody to which the words of the prayer are chanted is as impressive as the words themselves. 'We feel particularly aware as we listen to it,' they said, 'that this is happening in every Jewish community throughout the world.'

At Home Again

The family returned home from the synagogue after the Kol Nidre service, but of course they still observed the fast for Yom Kippur. Although they felt a little hungry, they had no intention of breaking the fast on this important annual occasion. They felt that if they did eat, it would be like telling God that they are not really sincere about saying 'sorry' for their wrong doing and that they do not really mean their resolve to do better in the future.

They told us that some Jews are so serious about Yom Kippur that they stay up all night and spend it in prayer.

Yom Kippur Day

Next day, the Goldbergs were up early and set off for the synagogue, without, of course, having any breakfast! We were reminded in the service about the festival story, since reading from the Torah included Leviticus 16 and Numbers 29 vv. 7-11 which tell about the Yom Kippur sacrifices in the days of the Temple.

We also heard words from the Prophet Isaiah 57 v. 14 to 58 v. 14. This passage begins with words which reminded us about the essential point of this festival: 'The Lord says, "Let my people return to me."' We had become fully aware that Yom Kippur and indeed, Rosh Hashanah which precedes it, is essentially about 'returning to the Lord' and deserting wrong doing. As we listened to the prophet's words, we were especially impressed by the following: 'The Lord says,

> The kind of fasting I want is this: Remove the chains of oppression and the yoke of injustice, and let the oppressed go free. Share your food with the hungry and open your homes to the homeless poor. Give clothes to those who have nothing to wear, and do not refuse to help your own relatives. Then my favour will shine on you like the morning sun, and your wounds will be quickly healed.'

An interesting feature of the afternoon worship was the reading of the Book of Jonah. The story of this short book from the Bible is that Jonah was sent by God to urge the people of the ancient Assyrian city, Nineveh, to repent of their wicked ways. Jonah did not want to go because he thought God's message was only for the Jews; he therefore took passage on a ship which would take him to a distant land. However, as you can read in the Book of Jonah, his attempt to escape from the task God had given him was in vain; he went to Nineveh and the result of his preaching was that the people fasted and prayed for forgiveness. This reading from Jonah reminded us that God's forgiveness is for everyone and not just for those of one faith or one race.

Yizkor

Anther impressive part of the afternoon worship on Yom Kippur was that known as **Yizkor** which means 'memorial service'. Jews believe that it is important to remember those who have died, so memorial prayers are offered and the worshippers are urged to remember the happy times shared with them when they were alive, and especially their good deeds which should be regarded as an example to follow. The worshippers mourning loved ones also pledged to give **Tzedakah**, i.e. a gift to charity, in memory of their loved ones.

Neilah

The final part of Yom Kippur worship in the synagogue takes place towards sunset and is called **Neilah**; that is a Hebrew word meaning 'closing'. Not only is this the closing worship of the festival, but many Jews refer to the idea that all through Yom Kippur they have prayed in the belief that the gates of Heaven are open to let their prayers in. As they remember Yom Kippur in the Temple days, they are reminded that at sunset the Temple gates were closed, and so they pray:

'O keep your gate open for us at the time of shutting the gate, for the day is nearly past. . . O grant that we may enter your gates. . .have mercy on us.'

The final acts in the whole service involved the reciting of the **Shema** by the whole congregation:

'Hear, O Israel, the Lord our God, the Lord is One. . .Blessed be his name, whose glorious kingdom is for ever and ever.'

This was followed by the words, repeated seven times: 'The Lord, he is God', as a firm declaration of resolve to follow sincerely the ways of God.

Last of all, there was a loud, long blast on the shofar. Many say that this is a reminder that the repentance they have

shown on Yom Kippur is something which they must continue throughout the whole year.

Task 1
The month Elul is seen as a time of preparation for Rosh Hashanah. What preparation is thought necessary? Why is it thought that preparation is necessary?

Task 2
The reading from the Torah on the first day of Rosh Hashanah is Genesis 22 vv. 1–19. Find that passage in a Bible and retell the story about Abraham.
    What religious lesson might it teach a Jew at the start of the ten days of repentance?

Task 3
Using the photograph on this page to help you, draw the shofar. What part does it play in the celebrations and the preparations for them?

Task 4
What do you consider is the value, if any, of an annual festival in which you repent and ask God's forgiveness?

Task 5
Explain the ideas behind the following symbols which are a part of Rosh Hashanah: white robes, Hallah bread, honey and apples, Tashlich.

Task 6
Imagine you were a visitor to Jerusalem centuries ago, witnessing the Yom Kippur ceremony; write an eye-witness account of it.

Task 7
Outline each of the various parts which make up the observance of Yom Kippur. Which of these do you find most impressive and contributing most to the spirit of Yom Kippur? Give reasons for your answer.

Sukkot and Simcha Torah

Five days after the fast of Yom Kippur, Jews are once again celebrating a festival. On this occasion it is the happy celebration of Sukkot which is the Hebrew word for 'booths'. This joyful festival lasts for nine days, the last of which is Simcha Torah, which means 'rejoicing in the Torah'.

Sukkot – The Festival Story

Centuries ago, the Hebrew people were slaves in Egypt but were led to freedom by Moses. The Bible tells how they wandered for forty years in the desert after leaving Egypt and had many adventures before finally reaching the land of Canaan where they settled.

During these years of wandering, they lived in 'tents' which were probably little more than makeshift shelters made of branches and possibly animal skins, or whatever similar materials were available. It was a very temporary kind of life, moving on from place to place, uncertain what lay ahead. There were times when they were very hungry and other times when they faced a very serious shortage of water; there was also the threat posed by hostile tribes they might meet on their travels and the anxiety about what kind of reception they would be given when they tried to move in and settle in Canaan.

It is this temporary life of their forefathers that Jews are especially remembering at the festival of Sukkot. It is also, however, a kind of harvest thanksgiving; indeed, in the Bible it is sometimes referred to as 'the festival of ingathering'. Certainly, once they were settled in Canaan, the Hebrews at the festival of Sukkot not only remembered the hard days of the desert journey, but also gave thanks to God for the gathering in of crops in their new land, for at this time of the year the grapes were ready to be made into wine and the crop of olives was ready to provide them with a plentiful supply of oil. Probably for these early settlers in Canaan, the contrast between the hard desert life and being able to reap a harvest was especially significant. It is hardly surprising that an annual festival to celebrate such a change became a regular feature of Jewish life.

The Celebrations

Sukkot is one of three Jewish festivals known as 'pilgrim festivals' because in the days of the Temple, Jews from various parts of the country would make a pilgrimage to Jerusalem to celebrate in the Temple. The other two are **Passover** and **Shavuot**.

The Sukkah
An important feature of this festival is that the Jewish family builds a **sukkah**: a little hut or shelter erected in the garden, the back yard or even on the flat roof of the house. The family spends as much time as possible in the sukkah for the period of the

The sukkah

very hard indeed; many also say that it is to remind them that, in the end, life is much more than material possessions which can fade away; they must depend on God who goes on for ever and never changes. Usually, part of the roof of the sukkah is left open so that, it is said, 'We may look up at the stars and direct our thoughts towards God.'

Some Jewish communities build a sukkah at the synagogue so that families who for various reasons cannot build one at home can share together in observing the festival. Our photographs were taken at such a synagogue sukkah.

Each evening during the festival when the table is set for the meal, it includes freshly baked Hallah bread, i.e. the plaited loaves which are always a part of the Sabbath eve meal. Also, as on the Sabbath table, there are candles and these are usually lit by the mother of the family as she recites a special blessing to mark the occasion.

festival and usually eats most meals in it.

Some families, after their meal at the end of Yom Kippur, before going to bed, put up the first post or drive in the first nail in the construction of the sukkah as a reminder that the festival of Sukkot has nearly arrived. Certainly in the few days between Yom Kippur and Sukkot, the whole family shares in the happy task of erecting the little shelter and decorating it with apples, grapes, pomegranates, indeed with any available colourful fruits and vegetables and with all kinds of flowers.

Although this shelter is beautifully decorated, it is intended to be a very fragile structure and the roof certainly would not keep out heavy rain. This is to remind the family that the life of their forefathers was

Guests

An interesting custom usually observed each day in the sukkah is to 'invite' one of the following great Biblical characters of the past – Abraham, Isaac, Jacob, Joseph, Moses, Aaron and David. When we asked Jews about this custom we were told that it reminds them of the part played in their history by these great men of long ago and it gives them a sense of belonging together, not only with fellow-Jews of today, but with all who have gone before over the many centuries.

The Four Species

The objects which Jacob is holding in the photograph are important in the festival of Sukkot. In his left hand is a citron which is a fruit rather like a lemon and it is known as the **etrog**; in his right hand is a palm branch known as the **lulav** and it is in a holder formed from a palm leaf; beside it are two willow branches and three myrtle branches.

The custom is in obedience to words in the scriptures – Leviticus 23 v. 40, 'You shall take on the first day, the fruit of goodly trees; branches of palm trees and boughs of leafy trees and willows of the brook, and you shall rejoice before the Lord your God seven days.'

On the first morning of the festival, Jacob stood facing towards the east and waved the lulav and etrog in front of him. Then he waved them on his right, to the south; over his shoulder, to the west; and on his left, to the north. As this was done he recited a blessing. This would be done each morning for the first seven days of the festival.

We questioned Jacob about this rather strange custom.

Our question: Jacob, to those of us who are not Jews, this seems a very strange practice: can you help us to understand it? First of all, why do you have a citron and the lulav?

Answer: Jews give many explanations, all

Etrog and lulav

of which suggest something important which we remember about our faith. This festival at one time probably marked the time when the final harvest of the year was complete and these objects would be symbols of that.

Others say that the lulav represents the spine; the myrtle is the eye; the willow represents the lips; and the etrog, the heart. Since in the ceremony these are all held together, they are reminding us that we should serve God with our whole being.

Some explain it this way: taste represents learning, smell represents good deeds; the etrog has taste and smell; the lulav has taste but no smell; the myrtle has smell but no taste; and the willow has neither taste nor smell! Each, therefore, represents a different kind of person; some have learning and good deeds, some have one or the other, and some have neither! But we hold these things closely together and this is saying that real fellowship is when all kinds of people are brought together to serve God.

Our question: Well, you certainly have convinced us that there is plenty of symbolism in the etrog and the lulav! Is this also true as far as the waving of these objects is concerned?

Answer: Yes, it certainly is. When we wave these, all four are held close together. Some say that each represents a letter of the four-letter name for God which looks like this in Hebrew:

When we wave them together we remind ourselves that the Lord our God is one God.

Since we wave in all four compass directions, we are declaring that God's presence is everywhere. Another view is that we wave them as an expression of joy and thanksgiving as we praise God at this happy festival time.

Sukkot in the Synagogue

There is worship in the synagogue on each day of the festival and the etrog and lulav play a part in the service on each of the first seven days, except on the Sabbath.

Part of the service is known as the **Hallel** and this consists mainly of chanting some Psalms. The etrogs and lulavs are waved especially as they come to words such as:

'O give thanks unto the Lord; for he is good: for his loving-kindness endureth for ever. O let Israel say that his loving-kindness endureth for ever.'

On the seventh day of the festival, which is known as **Hoshanah Rabbah**, Hebrew words meaning 'great help', there is a special celebration in the synagogue which includes a procession around the inside of the building seven times carrying the etrogs and lulavs; in addition, each person carries a small bunch of willows. Towards the end of the service, everyone took his bunch of willows and beat it on the pews until most of the leaves had fallen off!

Afterwards we asked about this custom and we were told: 'Several reasons are given for this ancient custom. Willows grow near water and it may be that our forefathers did something like that in the Temple as part of a ritual of prayer for rain. Certainly, even in our services today, we include prayers for rain and a continuing harvest. Most Jews, however, regard the beating of the willows as a symbol of their desire to 'beat off' their sins and so it is a reminder of the recent Day of Atonement when the emphasis was on the forgiveness of our sins.'

The Eighth Day

The eighth day of Sukkot is referred to as the Eighth Day of Solemn Assembly. The etrog and lulav are now laid aside. The synagogue service on this day is marked especially by memorial prayers for the dead and by a prayer called **Geshem**, which is a prayer for rain. One reason given for the prayer for rain is that, in Israel, spring crops depend on October rains. Since most Jews regard Israel as their homeland, they continue to offer this traditional prayer because they want their homeland to prosper.

Simcha Torah – The Festival Story

On the ninth day after the beginning of Sukkot comes one of the happiest celebrations of the Jewish year. On the occasion of Simcha Torah, young and old alike share in the festivities at the synagogue.

Simcha Torah does not have a story, as

such, behind it, since it does not really commemorate a historical event. It is a festival celebrating that book which is most important to Jews – the Torah. Every synagogue service includes readings from the Torah which is divided so that during the course of a year the whole of it will have been read. In other words, on any Sabbath in the year, a Jew will know which passage of the Torah will be read.

The Celebrations

On the eve of Simcha Torah, the synagogue was well filled, for this is always a very popular occasion. As you can see from the photograph, the Ark was open and the scrolls were lifted out and carefully carried by members of the congregation as they walked around the synagogue. Children followed carrying flags, and in this happy procession they circled the synagogue seven times.

At one point in the service, chapters 33 and 34 of the Book of Deuteronomy were read and this was followed by Genesis 1 v. 1 to 2 v. 3. This custom of reading both the end of one cycle of readings and the beginning of the next in the same service, has arisen according to some, 'to prevent Satan from accusing Israel that they were happy to finish the Torah (in the sense of getting it over with) and did not care to continue to read it!'

Morning Service

Next morning, the procession seven times around the synagogue was repeated with just as much joyousness as on the previous evening. There were, however, important new features in this service. A large **tallith** (i.e. a prayer shawl) was held out like a canopy across the **Bimah**, the platform from which the Torah is read; all the boys under thirteen years of age (i.e. all those not yet Bar Mitzvah) were called up. As they stood together under the tallith, they recited the words of a blessing. This is the one occasion in the year when boys who are not yet Bar Mitzvah are given the honour of being 'called to the Torah.'

An adult male member of the congregation was called up to read the last section of Deuteronomy. He is referred to as **Hatan Torah**, i.e. the bridegroom of the Torah; another was called up to read the beginning of Genesis: he is referred to as **Hatan Berayshis**, i.e. the bridegroom of the beginning. Simcha Torah has sometimes been likened to a wedding feast; certainly both these terms and the tallith being used as a canopy reminded us of a Jewish wedding. (See *Milestones* pages 77-82 for information on a Jewish wedding.) The idea behind this is that just as love is the keynote of a wedding, so love for the Torah is the keynote of Simcha Torah and indeed the keynote of the whole of life for a Jew. At a wedding, bride and bridegroom take each other to love for the rest of life; at Simcha Torah, the Jew remembers that he takes the Torah to love and obey for all of life; this is the book by which he lives.

The scrolls are carried round the synagogue

Task 1
Two of the occasions when the Israelite people complained to Moses, during their journey from Egypt, are related in Exodus 16 vv. 1-31 and 17 vv. 1-7; the first is when they were hungry, and the second when they faced a water shortage.

Choose one of these incidents and write a short play on it; include the conversation which might have taken place between those who complained and Moses. The final part of your play should be concerned with how the situation was resolved.

Task 2
Imagine a group of the Israelites who have recently settled in the land of Canaan; this is the land described to them as 'flowing with milk and honey'. They discuss among themselves their good fortune in settling here after their long journey from slavery in Egypt; they decide that they ought to hold an annual celebration. What might they have said in their discussion?

Task 3
If your family were Jewish where would you suggest your family sukkah should be erected? Describe what it would be like.

Task 4
What part is played by the following and what is their significance at Sukkot:
(a) inviting the 'holy guests'; (b) the etrog;
(c) the lulav; (d) the myrtle;
(e) the willow?

Task 5
Simcha Torah marks the end of one cycle of readings from the Torah and the start of another: do you see any value in the tradition of making sure that the whole of the holy book is read in a year? Give reasons for your answer.

Task 6
What does the happy celebration of Simcha Torah say about how the scriptures are regarded by Jewish worshippers?

Chanukah

About the end of November or the beginning of December each year, Jews celebrate the happy festival of Chanukah, which is sometimes referred to by the Hebrew words **Chag Haurim** which means 'festival of lights'. In the Jewish calendar the festival begins on the 25th day of the month Kislev.

The Festival Story

In the second century BCE, Judaea was part of the Syrian empire and in 175 BCE a new Syrian king became ruler. He was Antiochus IV, often known as Antiochus Epiphanes. Syria had been part of the wider Greek empire, and Greek influence, especially as far as religion was concerned, was very strong. Antiochus hated the Jewish people, mainly because they refused to accept the idol worship which he followed and insisted on being loyal to their own god whom they claimed was the only God. Antiochus ordered the Jews to give up their faith; this made them all the more determined to remain faithful to their God. Antiochus, therefore, sent his army to Jerusalem with orders to dedicate the holy Temple of the Jews to the Greek god, Zeus. Knowing that the pig is regarded as an unclean animal by Jews, he also had a pig sacrificed on the Temple altar. This, together with the placing of pagan images in the Temple, made it, as far as Jews were concerned, no longer a fit place to worship their God.

In the village of Modi'in, one of the King's officers arrived to enforce Antiochus's decree that all should worship the Greek gods. He ordered Mattathias, one of the leading men in the village, to take the lead and offer sacrifice to the pagan god. Mattathias refused but another Jew, fearing what might happen, said he would do so. Mattathias's anger blazed up and he struck down this man and the King's officer, killing them both. He then sent out a call for all who were loyal to their faith to follow him and fight for freedom. The resulting band of guerilla fighters included Mattathias's five sons, one of whom was Judas, who was to become the leader a few months later when his father died.

Judas became known as Judas Maccabaeus, i.e. Judas, 'the Hammer', because of the blows he struck for freedom. He and his followers continued the struggle against Antiochus and his army for three years and finally overcame them so that in 165 BCE Judas was able to lead his men triumphantly into the city of Jerusalem.

All were particularly concerned about the Temple, the place which, for them, was set apart for the worship of God. They were angry at the sight of images of Greek gods and goddesses in a place dedicated to the worship of their one God. They set about purifying the Temple of all these pagan influences and, by the twenty-fifth day of the month Kislev, the task was complete and a ceremony of rededication was held.

It is said that when they came to relight the lamp which was always kept burning just outside the most holy part of the Temple, they discovered that there was only enough holy oil, i.e. oil in a flask sealed with the seal of the High Priest, to keep it burning for one day. The story tells, however, that by some miracle it lasted for eight days and nights, by which time the priests had been able to produce a sufficient supply of oil fit for such a holy purpose.

So began the Jewish festival of Chanukah; this Hebrew word means 'dedication', i.e. giving over something to the purpose for which it was intended; at Chanukah, Jews remember the rededication of the Temple and the way in which good triumphed over evil.

The Celebrations

There are those who regard Chanukah as a minor Jewish festival because it looks back to an event which is not so ancient as, for example, that behind Passover. The story of Judas Maccabaeus comes not from the scriptures but from a collection of other important writings which are often known as the **Apocrypha**. In spite of this, most

Jews regard Chanukah as a happy festival which they love to observe. It is a particular favourite with children for there are many aspects of it which especially appeal to them.

Chanukah Candles
At this festival time you will find in a Jewish home a **menorah**, i.e. a candlestick; a seven-branched menorah is a common sight, especially in synagogues, where it stands as a reminder of the seven-branched, golden candlestick which was in the Jerusalem Temple. The Chanukah menorah, however, has nine branches, one of which stands apart from the rest. The festival lasts for eight days so there is one candle for each day, and the other, known as the **shammash** or 'servant candle', is used to light each of the others.

We visited the Rosenberg's home at Chanukah. They followed the custom of having a Chanukah menorah for each member of the family. We watched as they each lit the shammash, and then used it to light the first candle in the menorah and recited the blessing. We then asked Mr Rosenberg to tell us something about this aspect of the festival.

A Chanukah menorah

Second candle: Reflect on the victory of Judas and his followers over Antiochus.
Third candle: Reflect on the souls of those soldiers who gave their lives in the cause of freedom.
Fourth candle: Reflect on the plight of Jews in the Soviet Union.
Fifth candle: Reflect on the oppression of Jews in some Arab lands.
Sixth candle: Reflect on the struggle against bigotry and prejudice against Jews in many parts of the world.
Seventh candle: Reflect on the Jewish people's search for peace and freedom.
Eighth candle: Reflect on all who have been oppressed and pray that one day all nations, peoples and individuals will live in freedom and understanding with one another.'

Other Chanukah Customs
We learned of other customs which help to make Chanukah a very happy festival, especially for the children.

The Dreidel

'This festival,' he told us, 'lasts for eight days, so on the first day we light one candle, on the second, two, and so on until on the final day we light eight. A box of Chanukah candles contains forty-four; if you count up, you will find that to be the required number: one for the first day, two for the second, and so on, plus one shammash for each day.

'The Chanukah lights are for us to enjoy and are not to be used for anything. This is why we use the shammash to light the others, for the Chanukah candles are not even to be used to light another.

'There are some who suggest the following series of events on which we might reflect on each evening of Chanukah:
First candle: Reflect on Mattathias's brave action in the original Chanukah story and also on the refusal of Israel to lie down in the face of threats from her enemies.

There is a long-standing custom of playing games of chance during the evenings of Chanukah. The most popular of these is played with the **dreidel**. The dreidel is a kind of spinning top which is cube-shaped; there is a Hebrew letter on each of the four sides:

| Nun | Gimmel | Hey | Shin |

These are the first letters of the words

נֵס גָּדוֹל הָיָה שָׁם

which are pronounced 'Nes Gadol Hayah Sham' which means, 'A great miracle happened there.' The miracle which they remember as they play is the miracle of the Temple lamp.

There is a legend which says that the dreidel was invented at the time of Judas and his followers, who were known as 'the Maccabees'. Their enemy, King Antiochus, had ordered that no one must read the Torah, the scriptures of the Jews. In spite of this, groups of people did meet to study the Torah secretly. The legend tells how, when such groups met, a dreidel was laid on the table, and someone was posted to give warning of any approaching soldiers. If the lookout gave a warning, the Torah scroll was quickly hidden and the dreidel was spun; all that the enemy could see when they arrived was a group of Jews playing a game together!

To play the game, each player starts with the same number of pennies, matchsticks or some other kind of counters; each player puts one of these in the middle. The dreidel is spun by each player in turn; whether he wins or loses depends on which face of the dreidel is uppermost after it has been spun. If Nun is uppermost, the player does nothing; if it is Gimmel, the player takes everything in the middle; if it is Hey, the player takes half of what is in the middle; if it is Shin, he must put one of his counters into the middle. Before each player spins, everyone puts another counter into the middle.

Latkes
Food plays a part in most festivals and, in the case of Chanukah, one food which is universally popular among Jews is known as **latkes**. Mrs Rosenberg described how she made these: 'I take 3 large potatoes and, after peeling them, I grate them into a bowl; I do the same with a small onion. I then beat up 2 eggs which I add to the bowl together with 2 tablespoonfuls of flour and a little salt. This mixture should be reasonably stiff. I then drop it by spoonfuls into a well-oiled frying pan and fry on both sides. We eat these either with some apple sauce or sour cream. My family love to have these at Chanukah: I am sure you will enjoy them as well!'

We asked Mrs Rosenberg if she could tell us why these were specially associated with Chanukah. 'Various reasons are given,' she said. 'Some say that since they are cooked in oil, latkes should be another reminder of the oil that lasted for eight days in the story about Judas Maccabaeus. There is one tradition which links it with another story from the Book of Judith in the Apocrypha. According to the legend, Judith was from the same family as Mattathias; she killed one of the leaders of the enemies of the Jews by feeding him salty cheese until he was so thirsty that he drank too much wine. When he was drunk, she cut off his head!

'It is said by those who follow this tradition that latkes were originally made from cheese, and in this way, at Chanukah, they are remembering yet another blow which was struck for the freedom of our people.'

Dedication

We asked the Rosenberg family if they could sum up for us what Chanukah meant to them today. The children, of course, talked of the gifts, the games, the songs and the happy atmosphere in the home. Mr Rosenberg, however, while clearly enjoying all that, gave a more serious view of the festival.

'The name Chanukah,' he said, 'means "dedication"; as you have learned, we are celebrating the rededication of the Temple. It has been said that if the Maccabees had not risen up against Antiochus, our ancient faith would have disappeared and there would be no Jewish religion today. If that had happened, there would be no Christianity and no Islam either, for both of these faiths, at least to some extent, were born out of Judaism. We owe a great deal, therefore, to the heroism and faith of these great men in the past and we should dedicate ourselves to being faithful in our time. The outstanding feature of Chanukah is the lighting of the candles. Just as the light triumphs over the darkness because it is greater than the darkness, so we are reassured that good is stronger than evil and will overcome it.'

Task 1
Write a short play based on the festival story. Scenes could be as follows:
(i) Decree of Antiochus and news of the sacrifice of a pig reaching Modi'in.
(ii) Mattathias ordered to sacrifice and what resulted.
(iii) Triumph of Judas and lighting of Temple lamp.

Imagine the conversations which might have taken place and include these in your play.

Task 2
(a) Chanukah candlesticks are available in many designs; draw a design for your own Chanukah candlestick.

(b) Mr Rosenberg told us of some ideas for reflection on each evening of Chanukah; can you suggest eight ideas for reflection? Remember what lies behind the idea of light as a symbol.

Task 3
Here are instructions on how to make a simple dreidel:

You require a piece of strong cardboard 10 cm by 6 cm, a cocktail stick and some glue.

Mark out the card as shown below, with the four Hebrew letters on the middle row and diagonal lines drawn on each of the other squares.

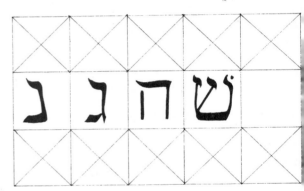

Carefully pierce a hole on each square where the diagonals cross, fold and cut the squares as necessary to form a little hollow box; the holes you have made should come together so that you can push the cocktail stick through. You should now be able to play the game as described. Can you suggest any variations on how it might be played?

Task 4
Chanukah means 'dedication'. What does dedication mean in relation to (a) a building, (b) an athlete or any sportsman or woman, (c) following a particular religious faith?

How far does the festival of Chanukah remind Jews that their faith demands dedication on their part?

54

Passover

It is the fifteenth day of Nisan in the Jewish calendar, which means that it is the first day of the Passover festival known in Hebrew as **Pesach**. The festival will last until the twenty-first of Nisan and during that whole period certain customs will be observed in every Jewish home. The festival is probably the best-known and perhaps the best-loved of all the festivals celebrated by Jews.

The Festival Story

We must go back nearly three and a half thousand years for the events celebrated at Passover! The Hebrew people, forefathers of the Jews of the present day, were slaves in Egypt and life for them was very hard indeed. It had not always been so: once, they had been the honoured guests of the Pharaoh, the king of Egypt, because they were the family of Joseph who had been of great service to the Pharaoh. (For the story of Joseph, see Genesis 37-50.)

At the particular time with which the Passover story is concerned, a Hebrew named Moses believed that God had called him to leave the land of Midian, where he had lived and worked as a shepherd, and go back to Egypt and gain the freedom of the Hebrew slaves. Moses, although a Hebrew himself, had been brought up as the son of the Egyptian princess, but had fled from Egypt after being involved in a serious incident which showed that his sympathies lay with the slaves. He had

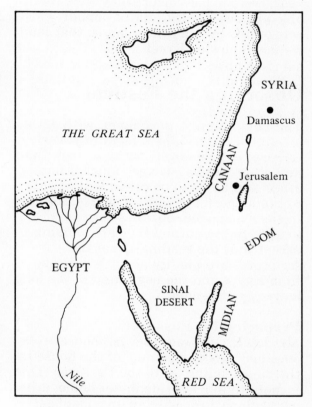

been away from Egypt for a very long time and there was now a different Pharaoh ruling Egypt.

Moses confronted the Pharaoh and asked him to let the slaves leave Egypt so that they could go and worship their God in freedom. The Pharaoh refused and made life even more difficult for the slaves. Eventually, a series of plagues hit Egypt.

Finally, there came the greatest disaster of all: in every Egyptian family the first-born son died. The Pharaoh, mourning for his own son, at last gave in and told Moses to lead the Israelites away as quickly as possible. Moses, expecting such a decision, had warned the people to be ready and, quickly, they all set off on their journey which soon led them into the desert. It was to become a very long journey indeed: forty years were to pass before they were finally able to move into the land of Canaan which was to become their new home; that land we now know as Israel.

Observing the Festival

The Levin family, in common with Jews all over the world, look forward eagerly to Passover. Passover, perhaps more than any other festival, is very much a family affair and tends to be celebrated mainly in the home. There are, of course, services in the synagogue, but these are very similar to the normal Sabbath worship except that the readings from the scriptures are mainly about the escape from Egypt and the beginning of the long journey to freedom.

Preparing for Passover

Mrs Levin, like most Jewish housewives, does her 'spring cleaning' of the house in the days leading up to the Passover. This is more than just pride in her home, it has particularly to do with an important aspect of Passover: that there will be no leaven in the home for the period of the festival. Leaven, or as Jews call it in Hebrew, **chametz**, is yeast or anything else which will cause dough to rise when it is baked. The custom of getting rid of any leaven for the festival is a reminder that when their forefathers escaped from Egypt and began the journey to freedom, it was with great haste and they had no time to wait for the dough to rise before baking their bread.

Search for Chametz

On the night of the 13th Nisan (to a Jew, the day begins at sunset, so it is, in effect, the start of the 14th Nisan), a symbolic search of the Levin's house was made. Mr Levin had a feather, a wooden spoon, a little cloth bag and a candle. When the whole family was together, the candle was lit and Mr Levin said the words of the traditional blessing:

'Blessed art thou, O Lord our God, King of the Universe,
Who has commanded us concerning the removal of leaven.'

Earlier, Mrs Levin had placed ten little pieces of bread on window-sills and shelves around the house. As Mr Levin found each one, he brushed it on to the spoon with the feather and put it into the bag; when all ten pieces had been found, spoon and feather were also put into the bag and put away till the morning.

Next morning, no chametz may be eaten after approximately 9.30 a.m., and about that time the family watched as the bag containing the bread, feather and spoon was burned.

Mr Levin told us that many Jews see this destruction of the leaven before Passover as more than just a symbol to remind them of the haste with which their forefathers left Egypt; it also serves as a reminder that they should search their lives and get rid of pride and live with greater humility.

For the eight days of the festival, no bread will be eaten in the Levin home; instead they will have **matzah** (plural: matzoth) i.e. unleavened bread which in appearance is rather like a water biscuit.

The Seder

On the first two evenings of the festival the Seder celebration is held in Jewish homes. **Seder** means 'order' and there is a set order for the celebration which is virtually the same whichever Jewish home

you may visit.

On the evening of 14th Nisan, all was ready in the Levin home for the first Seder of this Passover. The table had been carefully laid and Mr Levin gave us a 'conducted tour' of the items on the table, before the celebration began.

The Haggadah

He showed us a copy of a book which was at every place set on the table. 'This is the Haggadah,' he said, 'and it sets out the order we follow in our celebration of Passover. In fact, it has been described as a "guidebook" to Passover for it tells us how to prepare, it explains the symbols we use and it even has some Passover songs.'

Candles

There were two candles on the table: 'Shortly, my wife will light these,' he told us, 'and recite the words of a blessing, just as she does on the eve of every Sabbath. Once they are lit, the festival has begun in our home.'

Seder Dish

He pointed to a beautifully decorated plate on which there was a hard-boiled egg, a roasted lamb bone, some lettuce, a little parsley, horseradish and a mixture of chopped apples, nuts and cinnamon. Mr Levin explained the significance of these items: 'The roasted lamb bone represents the sacrifice of a lamb which used to be made at the Passover celebration centuries ago when we had the Temple in Jerusalem.

'The horseradish we call **moror**; it is also bitter in taste, and during the ceremony a little portion of it is eaten to symbolise the bitter suffering of our forefathers when they were slaves.

'We refer to the parsley as **karpas** and it symbolises the poor diet on which our forefathers existed when they were slaves. As part of the Seder meal it is dipped in the salt water which you see on the table; this is done as a remembrance of the tears which were shed by the slaves.

'The roasted egg symbolises the offering which was brought by all worshippers long ago when they came to the Jerusalem Temple to celebrate Passover. Many Jews see other ideas symbolised in it: for example, an egg is sometimes seen as a sign of mourning and it is said to commemorate the destruction of the Jewish Temple. Others say the Jewish people are like the egg: the more it is cooked, the harder it becomes; in the same way, the more we suffer persecution as Jews, the tougher we become and the more able to face such affliction as it comes.'

A Seder dish

It also reminds us of the lambs which every Israelite family had to slaughter and cook when they were making ready for their escape from Egypt in the time of Moses. The mixture of apples, nuts and cinnamon is called **charoset** and is supposed to resemble mortar as a reminder of the unhappy days of slavery in Egypt when the Israelite slaves were forced to make bricks and help with the Pharaoh's ambitious building programme.

'The lettuce is also such a reminder: just as lettuce tastes slightly sweet at first but leaves a bitter taste, so when we eat this we are being reminded that at first our forefathers were welcome in Egypt but later the Egyptians turned against them making their lives hard and bitter.

Wine

Also on the table was a decanter of red wine and at each place set for the ceremony was a wine glass. Mr Levin told us: 'At four different points in the Passover meal we drink a glass of wine. Wine figures in many Jewish celebrations and it is often said this is simply to mark it as a happy occasion. At Passover, it is said by many that four glasses are drunk to symbolise the four promises made by God according to the Book of Exodus 6 vv. 6-7: "I will bring you out. . .I will deliver you. . .I will redeem you. . .I will make you my own people." You will notice that there is an extra glass on the table; it will be filled with wine and kept on the table throughout the ceremony. It is known as "Elijah's cup"; according to Jewish belief, the Prophet Elijah will come to herald the coming of the Messiah, the one sent from God to bring peace to the world, and we remind ourselves of this particularly at Passover by having Elijah's cup ready, and by leaving the door ajar to symbolise the idea that Elijah may come and we are ready to welcome him. Really, this is our way of not only looking back to past events at Passover, but also looking forward with hope to a day of peace and brotherhood and love.'

The Ceremony

When all the family had gathered at the table on the evening of the 14th Nisan, the Seder ceremony was ready to begin. The candles were lit and Mr Levin began the ceremony by reciting various blessings which ended with the words:

'Blessed art thou O Lord our God, King of the Universe, who preserved us and sustained us and brought us to enjoy this season.'

After this blessing everyone drank their first cup of wine.

Mr Levin then washed his hands and gave a fragment of the karpas (parsley) dipped in the salt water to everyone present; after the recital of another blessing, all ate the karpas.

The middle piece of the three pieces of matzoth was taken, broken in two, one half replaced and the other hidden, to be eaten later on; this hidden piece is known as the **afikoman**.

The 'Bread of Affliction'

The next part of the ceremony is regarded by many as being at the heart of the Passover celebration. The matzoth was held up for all to see and Mr Levin began to read from the Haggadah:

'This is the bread of affliction that our fathers ate in the land of Egypt. All who hunger, let them come and eat; all who are in need, let them come and celebrate the Passover. Now we are here – next year we shall be in the land of Israel; now we are slaves – next year we will be free men.'

The Four Questions

It had previously been explained to us that this early part of the ceremony was presumed to have stimulated curiosity on the part of the younger members of the family, so the next part reflects that: the youngest child present recites four questions addressed to his or her father:

1 On all other nights we eat either leavened or unleavened bread. Why on this night do we only eat unleavened?
2 On all other nights we eat all kinds of herbs. Why on this night do we only eat bitter herbs?
3 On all other nights we do not dip the vegetables even once. Why on this night do we dip them twice? (This refers to dipping the parsley in the salt water, and later the bitter herbs in the charoset.)
4 On all other nights we eat either in a sitting position, or reclining. Why on this night do we all recline? (This refers to the

tradition that many Jews recline at the Passover table instead of sitting. The ancient world regarded reclining at table as a sign of being free. In many Jewish homes, the father at least reclines, supported by cushions, to carry on this Passover tradition.)

Mr Levin's youngest son asked these questions and his father replied by reading from the Haggadah the story of the escape of the Hebrew slaves from Egypt. At the point where he told of the plagues which fell on Egypt before the Hebrew slaves escaped, each member of the family dipped a finger in their cup of wine and flicked a drop on to the table at the mention of each disaster. We were told that the reason for this is that although the plagues brought about the escape of the slaves, they are nevertheless showing sadness in the face of human suffering. There were also various other readings from the Haggadah; at one point, Mr Levin raised his wine glass with the words:

'It is this divine pledge that has stood by our fathers and by us also. Not only one man has risen against us to destroy us, but in every generation have men risen against us to destroy us: but the Holy One (blessed be he!) always delivers us from their hand.'

We were told that many Jews today at this point think of the Holocaust, the slaughter of six million Jews by the Nazis. It was also pointed out to us that this statement is a great expression of faith in God: whatever the situation, God is looking after his people.

After the Haggadah readings had adequately answered the four questions, the second cup of wine was drunk as a kind of celebration and thanksgiving for the events remembered.

Eating the Matzoth

The words of another blessing were recited and everyone was given a piece of the unleavened bread to eat. This was followed by everyone having a small portion of the moror, dipped in the charoset; as they ate this, they were remembering the words from Exodus 1 v. 14 which told how the Egyptians made their lives bitter by using them as slaves and forcing them to work with mortar and bricks in their building projects.

Finally, before a full festival meal was served, everyone was given two little pieces of matzoth with some of the bitter herb between them. Once this had been eaten, they were all ready to enjoy the meal.

The Afikoman

After the meal, the Levin family followed the custom observed in most Jewish homes: Mr Levin had hidden the piece of matzah broken off earlier in the ceremony; now the young children searched for it. Rachel, the youngest daughter, soon found it and brought it to her father, who rewarded her, much to her delight. This piece, known as the afikoman, a word which means 'dessert', was broken up and all present had a share. As we watched, we felt that such an action as the hiding and finding of the afikoman made Passover not only a very serious occasion when important events from the past are remembered: it is also an occasion of happiness and fun.

Ending the Ceremony

As is the custom, 'grace' was said now that the meal was over. Mr Levin's words began:

'May the name of God be blessed from now on, and for ever. Blessed indeed be he of whose bounty we have eaten, and through whose goodness we live.'

All the family responded:

'Blessed be he and blessed be his name.'

This was followed by various other prayers of thanksgiving, after which the third cup of wine was drunk. Finally, some Psalms giving praise to God were recited before drinking the final cup of wine.

Table Songs
The whole celebration ended happily, with the family, much to the delight of the children, singing some traditional table songs specially remembered at Passover. One was about a goat, and ended:

> Then came God (blessed be he!)
> And smote the Angel of death
> Who slew the slaughterer
> Who killed the ox,
> That drank the water,
> That quenched the fire,
> That burned the stick,
> That beat the dog,
> That bit the cat,
> That ate the kid,
> That father bought for two coins,
> An only kid, an only kid!

As we looked back on this important Jewish festival, we could understand why it is so popular with the whole family, with its blend of the serious and sad mixed with happiness and fun; with its looking back to ancient history, but also its looking forward with faith in the goodness of God.

Task 1
Behind the festival story is the incident in which God called Moses to lead the Hebrew slaves to freedom. You can find this in Exodus 3 v. 1 to 4 v. 17.

Pick out the important points from this incident and write as if Moses were describing the experience and its effect on him. Note especially his reluctance to obey God's call.
or
Write in your own words the conversation between Moses and God which is part of the story told in the passage from Exodus.

Task 2
(a) Draw the Seder plate; label each item on it and explain what each symbolises.
(b) What part is played in the Seder meal by (i) matzoth, (ii) salt water, (iii) wine?

Task 3
Passover is a 'blend of the serious and sad mixed with happiness and fun'.
(a) Make a list of the part of the celebration which you think would be described as 'serious and sad' and those which you think express 'happiness' and appear to be 'fun'.
(b) Write a paragraph giving your views about whether a religious festival should be both serious and fun. Give reasons for your answer.

Task 4
When we talked with Mr Levin he told us he thought the Passover was a wonderful miracle of deliverance: celebrating it gave him hope for the future, faith in God, and it reminded him of the importance of freedom. Explain how you think the festival could convey such feelings to him.

Task 5
What answers might Mr Levin have given to the following questions:
(a) Why do you think it is important to remember an event which happened so many centuries ago?
(b) Why do you repeat the story each year?
(c) What words spoken during the ceremony express for you faith in God?
(d) We know that Jews over the centuries have observed the Passover even in times of grave danger such as the Holocaust. Do you think it is especially important to celebrate it at such a time?

62

Christian Festivals Introduction

Various branches of the Christian Church celebrate different festivals and there are many local festivals in different parts of the world which may be concerned, for example, with a particular saint associated with that area. We have chosen to deal only with the three universally celebrated festivals of Christmas, Easter and Whitsun. Although the content of these celebrations varies in different parts of the world, and even in different parts of Britain, all three, and the beliefs which lie behind them, are important parts of Christian life and worship wherever Christians are to be found.

The Christian Calendar

The calendar which governs Christian festivals is the one which is universally recognised and is called the **Gregorian calendar** because it was introduced in its present form by Pope Gregory 13th in 1582.

As far as the dates of festivals are concerned, Christmas is always 25th December, but Easter is variable, and since Whitsun follows seven weeks after Easter, it is also variable.

The date of Easter is fixed by tradition as the first Sunday after the full moon which occurs on, or next after, 21st March. This means that Easter can be as early as 21st March or as late as 25th April. This dating was an attempt to tie in Easter celebrations as closely as possible with the

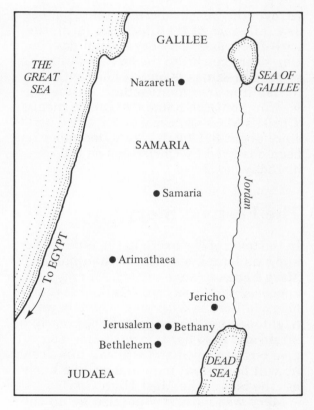

Jewish Passover, since the events in the life of Jesus being remembered at Easter took place at Passover time.

Most Christian Churches follow this tradition for the celebration of Easter, apart from that branch of the Church known as the Eastern Orthodox Church, who date their celebration by following a different, but also very old, tradition.

Christmas

All over the world, wherever there has been any influence of the Christian faith, the 25th December is a very special day, as Christians celebrate the birth of Jesus. For some, Christmas is only a holiday, a time for families to come together, a time for feasting; but the name *Christmas* means 'Christ's Mass' or 'Christ's Festival' and since about 350 CE the 25th December has been observed by Christians as the birthday of Christ.

The Festival Story

In the town of Nazareth in the land we now know as Israel, a young woman named Mary had a strange vision. An angel appeared to her saying, 'Hail, O favoured one, the Lord is with you!' She felt very frightened but the angel told her not to be afraid and gave her this message. 'You will give birth to a son and will call him Jesus; he will be a great man and will be known as "the Son of the Most High God".'

Mary was naturally puzzled by all this since she was not even married! She was, however, 'betrothed' to be married to a man named Joseph. 'Betrothed' was like being engaged but was much more binding.

Mary's vision continued with the angel telling her that the power of God would come upon her to create the child so that he would be called 'holy, the Son of God.'

Several months later, it was announced that the Romans, who occupied the land at the time, were to hold a census, and people must travel to the chief town for their own particular tribe. This meant that Mary and Joseph had to travel from Nazareth to Bethlehem which lay just over one hundred miles to the south.

Bethlehem was, of course, extremely busy because of the census, and Mary and Joseph could find nowhere to stay. Joseph was very anxious indeed because Mary's baby was nearly due to be born. In desperation, he accepted the offer of a corner in the stable close to the inn and there Mary's child was born.

Shepherds

In the fields outside Bethlehem, a group of shepherds were sitting, idly chatting as they kept watch over their flocks. Suddenly, the whole night scene was a blaze of light as they shared the vision of an angel who brought the message to them, 'Don't be afraid; I bring you good news of great joy, for to you is born today in Bethlehem, a Saviour, the Messiah, the Lord! You will find him lying in a manger.' When the shepherds recovered from the shock of this they set off to the town and discovered that it was all true.

The Wise Men and Herod

Meanwhile, in another place, wise men who studied the stars had seen a new star appear in the sky and were convinced that it marked the birth of someone special. They set out to follow the star and it brought them to the palace of King Herod the Great in Jerusalem.

The Christmas crib

The Celebrations

A Postman's View

Herod was very troubled by all this for he felt his position as king might be threatened. However, he did not share his fear with the wise men but sent them on their way to Bethlehem, saying, 'When you find the child, come back and tell me, so that I can worship him also.'

The wise men did find the child and they bowed down before him, offering gifts of gold, frankincense and myrrh. They did not return to Herod for they had a dream which warned them that he intended some evil. Joseph also had a dream which warned him and, as a result, he took Mary and the child to Egypt where they lived for about two years before returning to live in Nazareth where Jesus was to grow up.

Herod was furious and, in a fit of mad rage, ordered the killing of any male children born in and near Bethlehem around the time of the wise men's visit.

One of those to whom we talked some days before Christmas was Mr Lees who works as a postman.

'Christmas is a very busy time for me,' he said, 'for the amount of letters, greetings cards and parcels at this time is enormous. It is, however, a very happy time, and usually when I am delivering Christmas mail, people are especially friendly. The greetings cards are from friends and members of the family and this is one of the ways in which people keep in touch at this happy festival.

'I always remember some years ago delivering some cards to two ladies who were chatting together on the doorstep and, as I walked away, heard one saying to the other, as she opened the envelopes and looked at the cards, "I do hate these religious Christmas cards!" I have often thought about these words, for if Christmas is the birthday of Christ, how can it be anything else but a religious celebration? We seem, however, to have made it more of a pagan celebration, where it is merely a case of a holiday when families meet together, give each other gifts, eat and drink a great deal and enjoy happy parties. It is not that I dislike such aspects of Christmas! I am just rather sad that at the birthday of Christ, so many should forget what the festival is really all about.'

The Christmas Crib

We met a lady who was helping to set out a Christmas crib, some weeks before Christmas. This is a scene depicting the stable at Bethlehem, which is on view at a central point in her town near one of the churches. It portrays the baby Jesus, lying in a manger, in a shed strewn with straw and surrounded by the figures of Mary, Joseph, the shepherds and the wise men.

We asked the lady how she thought of Christmas and she told us, 'I think it is important for people to be reminded of what is at the heart of this festival. I am happy to help set up this scene so that, as folk are busy shopping for gifts and the food which is such an important part of Christmas, they can also see this simple nativity scene and remember that we are really celebrating the birthday of Christ. Christians regard this as the most important event of all time – God becoming flesh – God coming to live our kind of life. That, for me, is what Christmas is about.'

We expressed the view that perhaps the stable at Bethlehem was not really like this nativity scene she was helping to set out. 'Does that really matter?' she replied. 'This scene reminds us of the essentials – the humblest of surroundings, the mother and father who were simple ordinary folk, and the visitors who recognised the importance of this baby who had been born. It reminds me that God is concerned with ordinary folk like you and me.'

Carol Singers

During the week before Christmas, we came across a group of young people from one of the churches in the community who were going round the streets singing carols. As we approached we heard the words

'O come, all ye faithful, joyful and triumphant,
O come ye, O come ye to Bethlehem.
Come and behold Him, born the King of angels,
O come let us adore Him, Christ the Lord.'

We talked with some of the older people among them to discover why they were out on such a cold evening, singing these songs around the district. They reminded us that singing carols is a very old custom and they felt sure that since these were very happy songs about one of the happiest events the world has ever known – the birth of Christ – people would be glad to hear them.

We noticed some of the group had collecting boxes and were calling at the houses nearby. When we enquired about these we were told that they had decided to collect for Christian Aid, a charity which aims to help needy people in many places throughout the world. 'Christmas is a time of giving and receiving gifts,' they said, 'and we feel that we are very fortunate compared with people in many places who never have one decent meal, never mind the kind of Christmas dinner we will have! We feel that Christ himself and his parents were a bit like refugees – nowhere for him to be born except the stable – and so when we collect to give to needy people, it is as if we are giving gifts to him.'

A Happy Christmas!

We were invited to meet with a church youth group who, with their Minister, were discussing Christmas. We took the opportunity to put some questions to them.

66

Our question: You have been discussing the real meaning of this festival and we have heard you express the view that it is only a truly Christian festival when we sincerely remember the birth of Christ and all that his coming to the world has meant. Do you think all the other aspects of Christmas as it is now celebrated should be abolished, or at least ignored as far as Christians are concerned? Has the Christmas tree, decorations, parties, special food, Father Christmas and all the rest of the Christmas scene any value for you?

Answer: O yes! We would not like all that to disappear! After all, a birthday is a happy event and why not have a party to celebrate Christ's birthday? In our discussions about Christmas, we have learned that the 25th December was originally a pagan festival. The Romans had a holiday at that time of the year when they honoured Saturn; early sun worshippers, it seems, also celebrated at this time. Customs like lighting candles and giving gifts were probably a part of these; Christians took over the festivals and, instead of honouring Saturn or the sun, they honoured Christ, but they also kept some of the happy parts of the celebrations like giving gifts, lighting candles and feasting.

Christmas Eve Worship

A Christingle Service

There was a service in one of the churches in our community called a 'Christingle Service', which was mainly intended for children. We were told there would be some of the popular Christmas carols, a few short readings from the Christmas story in the Bible, then all the children present would be given a 'Christingle'. We were curious to know what a Christingle was!

Our curiosity was satisfied as we saw the children come out to the front of the church and a Christingle was given to each one: it was an orange with a little candle placed on the top; small cocktail sticks had been put in around the orange and each had raisins and nuts on it; around each orange was tied a red ribbon.

The Minister explained about the Christingle to the children in the service. 'The round orange is a symbol of the world; the candle is a symbol of Jesus whom we often call "the Light of the world" and it is his coming into the world that we are celebrating at this Christmas time. The fruit and the nuts are a reminder of the fruits of the earth and we thank God for these; lastly, the red ribbon is a reminder of the blood of Christ, for although we are

now celebrating his birth, we also remember that he died on the Cross for us.'

A Christingle

Christmas Communion
Most Christian churches have another act of worship, much later on Christmas Eve, which goes on into the beginning of Christmas Day. It may have different names according to which Christian tradition it belongs: it may be known as the First Communion of Christmas, or Christmas Eucharist, or Midnight Mass. At this service there are usually Christmas carols, readings from the Christmas story and then the climax of it is communion — eating bread (or wafer) and drinking a little wine as a way of remembering not only the birth of Christ but also his death.

An Impression of Christmas Communion
We talked to a young person who had been present at this part of Christmas worship, for we were curious to know what impression it made. Here is what we were told:
'We arrived at the church for the service which was to begin at 11.30 p.m. The church looked splendid, for, in addition to the candles on the altar, there were many other candles on window-sills and on the ends of pews; there was a beautiful Christmas tree which was also covered in coloured lights which reflected off the silvery tinsel draped over it. The church was full as the Minister entered and the service began.

'We sang many of the usual Christmas carols and listened to the familiar Bible readings retelling the story of the birth of Jesus. There were prayers in which we gave thanks for the coming of Jesus and in which we prayed for all those people who would not have the happy Christmas we were enjoying.

'I glanced at my watch and saw that it was now just past midnight: Christmas Day had dawned! My mind wandered to thoughts of Christmas when I was quite young: the excitement and anticipation of waking up on Christmas morning and the feeling of "magic" in the air! What had Father Christmas brought me? What other gifts would I receive? I came back to the present as I heard the voice of the Minister saying something about Christ dying. I realised that we had now moved into the communion part of the service. Before long the worshippers were filing out to kneel at the altar and receive bread and wine, with the words, "the Body of Christ," "the Blood of Christ". I suppose it was the atmosphere of the church that made me think so seriously, but I began to ask questions in my own mind: here we are supposed to be thinking of the birth of someone very special, and we are talking about his death! I looked around me and it was obvious that the majority of those present found the whole experience quite moving.

'Our worship ended with the singing of the carol, "O Come All Ye Faithful," and we sang the last verse especially with feeling at this early hour of Christmas

Christmas communion

morning:

Yea, Lord, we greet thee,
Born this happy morning,
Jesus, to thee be glory given;
Word of the Father,
Now in flesh appearing:
O come let us adore him,
O come let us adore him,
O come let us adore him, Christ the Lord!

'I enjoyed the carol, but it sparked off another question in my mind – "Word of the Father, now in flesh appearing" – what does that mean?'

Questions Answered

After Christmas, we pursued the questions raised by that young man's impression of the first communion of Christmas and discussed them with the Minister.
Our question: We would like to put our young friend's last question to you first of all. He wondered what was meant by the words in the carol, 'Word of the Father, now in flesh appearing'. Is there something important here which Christians believe about the event celebrated at Christmas? *Answer:* Yes, there certainly is, and I will try to explain it simply without getting involved in too much theological language! In the Gospel according to John, in the New Testament, there is no account of the birth of Jesus, but it does use the expression 'the Word' and it clearly means Jesus; it says, 'before the world was created, the Word already existed. . . through him God made all things'. Then later it says, 'the Word became a human being and. . .lived among us'.

One way of interpreting this is to say that 'the Word' means 'God in action' and Christians believe that in the human life of Jesus, God himself was speaking, not in mere words, but in action. So these words of the carol, 'Word of the Father, now in

69

flesh appearing' really mean that God the Father has himself come to speak to people in the flesh, in the human life of Jesus, and he is speaking not just in words but in actions. The common expression, 'Actions speak louder than words' is certainly true in this case!

Our question: What about the thought, 'Should we really be dwelling on the death of Christ when we are celebrating his birth?' Is that not somewhat strange and even morbid?

Answer: No, not at all! Though I do understand it being asked. Do you remember that we had the same idea being symbolised in the Christingle service? The red ribbon around the orange was a reminder that Christ died for us. Here in Communion, even as we welcome the birth of Jesus, we remember his death. You see, we believe it is important not to put aspects of the life of Christ into little compartments. The Christ who was born at Bethlehem is the same Christ who died on the Cross, and those events, and everything that happened in between, is summed up in one belief which Paul, in 2 Corinthians 5 v. 19 expresses in the words, 'God was making all mankind his friends through Christ.' So the birth of the child at Bethlehem in the humblest possible way, was God reaching out in friendship and love, but so was Christ's death, which was saying, in effect, 'Look, I am prepared to go this far to prove my love!' We do not want Christmas to be a sentimental 'cooing' over a sweet little baby born in a manger, but rather a celebration of the God who comes to us in friendship and love at Bethlehem and at the Cross, and every day in our individual lives.

Our question: Is that what you mean also when you talk of Christ as 'the Light of the world'?

Answer: Yes, indeed! Light gets rid of darkness, and we believe Christ works to get rid of the darkness of evil in our lives and in the world. On the day he was born,

a light was lit which has never gone out and not even when men tried to destroy him on the Cross could they do so, for God raised him from the dead and his light of truth and goodness still shines on.

Task 1
You can read for yourself the stories of the birth of Jesus in Luke 1 vv. 26-38 and Matthew 1 v. 18 to 2 v. 16. Read these through and then attempt the following:

(a) List everything from the stories which suggests the idea that this was the birth of someone very special indeed.

(b) What is there to suggest that the message of Christmas is for the ordinary people as well as for the great?

(c) If there had been such things as radio or television at the time of the birth of Jesus, how might the news of this event have been presented?

Task 2
Make a list of the ways in which Christmas is often celebrated today, e.g. the giving of gifts. Try to explain what each celebration you have listed contributes to Christmas as a religious festival and how it relates to the story of Christ's birth.

Task 3
Conduct a class discussion on the topic, 'Abolish all frivolity and money-wasting activities at Christmas!'

Task 4
Draw a Christingle and explain what each part symbolises.

Task 5
The postman overheard a woman saying, 'I do hate these religious Christmas cards!' What kind of Christmas cards do you think would have appealed to her? Draw or describe various types of Christmas cards you have seen. For each one state what you think it contributes to the meaning of the festival.

Easter

If any one festival is more important than another, certainly Easter must be the most important to Christians since this is a festival which remembers the death and rising again of Jesus and so much that Christians believe depends on this.

Christians often refer to the week which begins with Palm Sunday and leads up to Easter Day as **Holy Week** because the events they are remembering are so important to them.

Palm Sunday procession

Palm Sunday –
The Festival Story

Jesus of Nazareth, the young Jewish man who had been making such an impression on many people by his teaching and healing in various districts of Galilee and Judaea over the last three years, was now heading for Jerusalem. His disciples were rather anxious for they felt that he was going to walk into trouble in the city since he had made many enemies by his outspoken teaching. Jesus, however, was quite determined that he had to go and face whatever lay ahead.

One Sunday, Jesus and his disciples had reached the outskirts of Bethany, a little village close to Jerusalem. Here, he gave instructions to two of his men to go into the village where they would find a donkey tied up. They were to bring it to Jesus and, if anyone questioned their action, they were to say, 'The Master needs it and will send it back at once.'

The donkey was brought and the disciples placed cloaks on its back and helped Jesus to mount. Soon a little procession set off towards the city. As they proceeded, the number of followers grew and some in the crowd took off their cloaks and laid them in the path of Jesus; others fetched branches from nearby trees and laid them like a carpet in the road ahead of him. Some began to shout and soon the cry was taken up by the majority of the crowd, 'Hosanna! Blessings on him who comes in the name of the Lord!'

So the procession reached the city with Jesus being welcomed as a king! Clearly the feeling in the crowd was that this must be the Messiah, the One they believed God was going to send to lead them into a new era of peace and prosperity.

The Celebrations

In the majority of Christian churches throughout the world, this Sunday before Easter is celebrated as the **Palm Sunday** festival. If you were fortunate enough to visit Jerusalem on this day you would see a procession of Christians following the route which it is believed was taken by Jesus from Bethany into the city itself.

In our community, the churches celebrate this festival in their services of worship. In the service we attended, the Minister reminded the congregation that Jesus' ride into Jerusalem was a 'sermon without words'. By coming in this humble way he was saying, 'Look, this will help you understand the kind of person I am and the kind of king I am!'

The other important part of our community's celebration of Palm Sunday was a 'procession of witness'. After the

services in the various churches, people met together and walked through the streets in procession. At the head of the processsion was a donkey, a reminder of that procession in Jerusalem so long ago. In addition, one of the ladies carried baskets of 'palm crosses' and she gave these to people whom she met as the procession passed through the district. **Palm crosses** are small crosses made from strips of palm leaves and they serve two purposes: they are reminders of the people of Jerusalem welcoming Jesus by laying palm branches in his path; they also remind of a more solemn fact, that five days later, Jesus was put to death on a cross and that cross has become the most important symbol in all Christianity.

As they walked in procession, some of the time they sang hymns which were particularly about Palm Sunday. One of these reminded, just as the palm crosses did, that this joyful day for Jesus was soon to be followed by his death:

'Ride on, ride on in majesty!
In lowly pomp ride on to die!
O Christ thy triumphs now begin
O'er captive death and conquered sin.'

Maundy Thursday – The Festival Story

The Thursday of Holy Week is often referred to as **Maundy Thursday**. This name comes from the Latin word 'mandatum' which means 'that which is commanded' and refers to the command which Jesus is said to have given to his followers at this time, that they must love one another.

Jesus spent a great deal of time in the city of Jerusalem during the week that followed Palm Sunday. On the Thursday evening he wanted to share with his disciples a meal associated with the festival of Passover (see pages 55-62).

Jesus knew that his enemies were plotting against him so his plans for this meal were made secretly and in the evening he and his twelve disciples met in an upper room which had been made ready. As the meal progressed, the disciples realised that Jesus was giving some new meaning to it which, at the time, they could not really understand. He took bread, broke it in pieces and, as he passed it to his disciples, said, 'This is my body, given for you.' After this he took a cup of wine and, when he had taken a sip from it, passed it round the others with the words, 'This is my blood shed for many; drink this and remember me.'

Also on this occasion, Jesus told the disciples that one of them would betray him to his enemies and that they would all let him down by running away. They were shocked by this and swore their loyalty to him. When his disciple, Peter, said, 'The others may run away but I never will,' Jesus told him that on that very night, even he would disown him three times.

From this strange meal together, they all went out to the Garden of Gethsemane at the foot of the Mount of Olives and there, Jesus was arrested by his enemies.

The Celebrations

For many Christians, the evening of Maundy Thursday is a special occasion when they meet and, as part of their worship, re-enact the last supper which Jesus shared with his disciples.

In some churches the priest may wash the feet of a few members of the congregation in remembrance of the fact that at the Last Supper, Jesus washed the disciples' feet, taking on the role of a lowly servant. Those Christians who do this say that it is a reminder that they are called to be servants of others and should serve with humility.

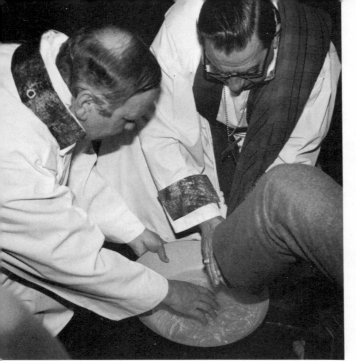
Foot washing

One member of the church which we visited for this occasion told us, 'This is, of course, not the only time when we take Communion, as we call this particular act of worship; but it always seems special when we are particularly thinking of the events in the last week of Jesus' life before he was crucified. We find ourselves picturing that scene in the upper room and, as we take the bread and the wine, find ourselves wondering how much we would have understood if we had been there. Many of us also ask ourselves if we would have been any more loyal to him than the disciples were on that Thursday evening.'

Good Friday – The Festival Story

On the Thursday evening, after Jesus was arrested, he was taken before a hastily called meeting of the Sanhedrin, the Jewish court. He was accused of speaking against God – the court called it 'blasphemy'; his enemies wanted him dead, however, so it was decided to bring him before the Roman governor, Pontius Pilate, next morning, for he alone could order such an execution.

When Jesus appeared before Pilate, the governor could find no real evidence on which to convict and sentence him; he felt, however that there were those who might send reports to the Roman emperor about him if he took no action; then he remembered a custom that at Passover time the governor could offer to pardon a notable prisoner, so he offered the people the choice – Jesus, or Barabbas, who was probably awaiting execution for treason. To his surprise, the crowds shouted for Barabbas and he had no choice but to order the crucifixion of Jesus.

On that Friday morning about 9 o'clock, Jesus was led out to the place of execution, nailed to a wooden cross and left to die. Just after 3 o'clock it was all over; his body was taken down from the cross and laid in a tomb given by one of his friends, called Joseph from Arimathaea.

The Celebrations

Good Friday is a very special day for Christians since they remember the death of Jesus on the cross. Many churches have a service which begins at 12 noon and goes on until 3 o'clock, to remind the worshippers of the final three hours during which Jesus suffered on the cross. In some there is a particularly stark reminder by the holding up of a crucifix in full view of the congregation. In such a service in our community, the hymns which were sung were obviously about Jesus' death. One very well-known one was:

'There is a green hill, far away,
Outside a city wall;
Where the dear Lord was crucified,
Who died to save us all.'

Besides such hymns being sung and readings from the Bible telling the story of Jesus' death, there were many periods of silence when the congregation had the opportunity just to sit and think about the death of Jesus. Everything in church fitted such a solemn occasion: the Vicar was wearing his black cassock, without the usual white surplice; there were no flowers in church as there usually are, and the altar had no coloured cloth on it as it has for the normal Sunday services.

This was a very moving occasion as the congregation was reminded of Christians all over the world thinking together of the death of Jesus and celebrating this as the way in which, they believed, God's love for people was being shown.

Easter Day – The Festival Story

Early on the Sunday morning, three women made their way to the tomb of Jesus. The Jewish Sabbath was now over and they wanted to anoint the body of Jesus as was their custom. Imagine their surprise when they found that the stone had been rolled away from the entrance to the tomb and, when they looked inside, they saw that the body was no longer there. Later, they told a story of a vision of a young man sitting inside the tomb who said to them, 'Don't be afraid, you are looking for Jesus of Nazareth who was crucified. He has risen; he is not here; look, there is the place where they laid him. But go and give this message to his disciples: "He will go before you into Galilee and you will see him there!" ' Sometime after, Jesus appeared to a number of his friends and disciples in various places and they were all convinced tht it really was him and that he had risen from the dead.

The Celebrations

The Easter Vigil
In many churches the celebration of Easter Day begins on the Saturday evening with a ceremony known as 'the Easter Vigil'. We went to a Roman Catholic church for this impressive service.

When we arrived at the church it was in darkness and we gathered with the rest of the congregation outside where a fire had been lit in a brazier. The priest came and stood by the fire and one of his assistants stood beside him carrying a very large candle. The members of the congregation had each been given a small candle which was later to be lit.

The priest began by saying:

Dear friends in Christ, on this most holy night, when our Lord Jesus Christ passed

Kindling the fire

from death to life, the Church invites her children throughout the world to come together in vigil and in prayer. This is the passover of the Lord: if we honour the memory of his death and resurrection by hearing his word and celebrating his mysteries, then we may be confident that we shall share his victory over death and live with him for ever in God.

This was followed by a prayer of blessing over the fire:

Father, we share in the light of your glory through your Son, the light of the world. Make this new fire holy, and inflame us with new hope. Purify our minds by this Easter celebration, and bring us one day to the feast of eternal light. We ask this through Christ our Lord. Amen.

The large Easter candle was brought to the priest and he was handed a stylus. The candle was marked with the shape of a cross; above this was the Greek letter Alpha, and below it the letter Omega; between the arms of the cross he drew the numerals of the year. As he did this he sai

Christ yesterday and today
The beginning and the end
Alpha
and Omega
all time belongs to him,
and all the ages;
to him be glory and power
through every age and for ever.
Amen.

The Greek letters Alpha and Omega are the first and last in the alphabet and are used to symbolise the idea that Christ is the beginning and the ending of all that gives life meaning.

Next, the priest inserted five grains of

incense into the candle in the shape of a cross, with the words:

> By his holy and glorious wounds, may Christ our Lord guard us and keep us, Amen.

Then the candle was lit from the fire with the words,

> May the light of Christ, rising in glory, dispel the darkness of our hearts and minds.

Procession

A procession moved towards the church led by the priest carrying the lighted Easter candle and chanting, 'Christ our Light'. The congregation all responded by chanting, 'Thanks be to God'. As he reached the church door, the priest lifted the candle high so that all could see it and again he chanted, 'Christ our Light'. Again, the congregation responded in the same way as before.

As we all took our places in the pews inside the church, our candles were lit by tapers which had been lit from the Easter candle. It was a most impressive sight to see so many flickering candles held by the large congregation which had come to keep this Easter vigil.

When the priest placed the large Easter candle by the altar, he turned and faced us chanting for a third time, 'Christ our Light'. Again came the response, 'Thanks be to God,' and at that point the whole church became a blaze of light as all the lights were switched on.

Marking the Easter candle

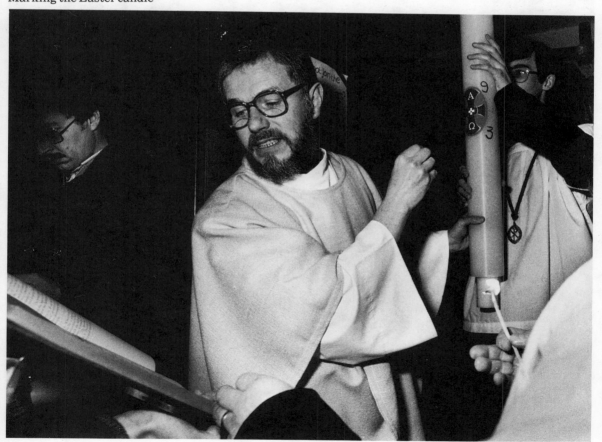

(top) Procession into the church   (bottom) 'Christ our light'

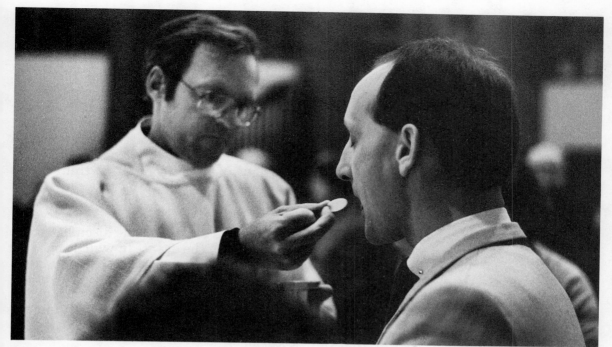

'The Body of Christ'

The Word of God

Later in the service there were readings from the Bible; the first was from Genesis 1 v. 1 and vv. 26-31, which reminded all of the ancient story of the creation of the world.

These Bible readings were followed by the congregation reciting words known as the **Gloria**:

Glory to God in the highest,
and peace to his people on earth.
Lord God, heavenly King,
Almighty God and Father,
We worship you, we give you thanks,
We praise you for your glory.
Lord Jesus Christ, only Son of the Father,
Lord God, Lamb of God,
You take away the sins of the world:
Have mercy on us;
You are seated at the right hand of the Father:
Receive our prayer.
For you alone are the Holy One,
You alone are the Lord:
You alone are the Most High,

Jesus Christ,
With the Holy Spirit,
In the glory of God our Father.
Amen.

Communion

The final act of worship at this Easter vigil was Communion, or the **Mass**, as it is called in Roman Catholic churches. Many members of the congregation filed out to kneel at the altar where the priest gave each one a small white wafer, with the words, 'The Body of Christ'. In this way the Christians were all reminded of the events of Good Friday, when Christ died on the cross.

The service ended just after midnight, when Easter Day had dawned, with the whole congregation singing a happy Easter hymn.

As we left the church, the flame of the large Easter candle still burned steadily; it would remain lit for every service held during the next seven weeks until the festival of Whitsun.

Easter Day

All Christian churches celebrate the resurrection of Jesus with special acts of worship on Easter Day (Easter Sunday). We returned to the church which we visited on Good Friday: what a transformation! The church which then had seemed bare with no flowers and no altar cloth was now decorated with many spring flowers and the altar was covered with a white, richly embroidered cloth; the Vicar, too, looked splendid in his richly coloured robes.

The service was a very happy one with the joyful Easter hymns being sung, such as, 'Jesus Christ is risen today, Hallelujah!'

During the service the Vicar talked to the children who were present. He held up a very big chocolate Easter egg and used it to focus the children's attention on what Easter is really all about. He said that the English name for this festival, 'Easter', is said to come from the name of an Anglo-Saxon goddess, Eostre, who was worshipped in Britain many centuries ago. She was a goddess of spring and it is thought that at one time eggs were given as a symbol of new life at the time of a spring festival in her honour and as a way of giving thanks for the rebirth of growing things after the long winter. Since Christ's death and resurrection took place in springtime, Christians took some of the old customs and gave them new meaning related to their faith in Jesus Christ.

Some, he said, think of the Easter egg as a reminder of the stone rolled away from the tomb of Jesus, but he wanted them especially to think of it as a symbol of the new way of life which Jesus had made possible by his death and rising again.

The Vicar finished by saying that although the festival of Easter with its Easter eggs only comes once a year, every Sunday is Easter for the Christian because they remember that Jesus rose from the dead on the first day of the week and he helps them live their lives in a better way.

Task 1
In the service on Palm Sunday, the Minister described Jesus' entry to Jerusalem as 'a sermon without words. By coming in this way he was saying, "This will help you understand the kind of person I am." '

What kind of person do you think Jesus was suggesting he was on this occasion?

Task 2
Imagine you are one of the disciples: write an account of the events in which you were involved with Jesus on (a) Good Friday, and (b) Easter Sunday. (You can read the Biblical accounts of (a) in Luke 22, v. 66 to 23 v. 56 and of (b) in Luke 24.) Include a description of your feelings on both occasions.

Task 3
Draw the Easter candle and explain the significance of its symbols.

Task 4
Make a chart of the Holy Week services, set out as follows:

Service	Occasion being remembered	Symbols which illustrate or remind of the occasion

Task 5
Easter is usually regarded as the most important of the Christian festivals: why do you think this is so?

If Christians did not believe in the events celebrated at Easter, how might this change the way in which they regard Jesus?

Whitsun

Seven weeks after Easter comes the festival of Whitsun. Sometimes it is called by the name of the Jewish festival, 'Pentecost'; it is often referred to as 'the Birthday of the Church'.

The Festival Story

It was the Jewish festival of Pentecost, or to give it its Hebrew name, 'Shavuot', the Feast of Weeks, which celebrated the harvest of the first fruits of the crop of barley which were about to be collected. This was a particularly important festival in Judaism for it also marked the giving of the Law to Moses on Mount Sinai. Many called it 'Pentecost' (a Greek word meaning 'fiftieth') because it occurred fifty days after the Passover Festival.

The temple precincts were crowded with pilgrims who had come to offer sacrifices

to God. The disciples of Jesus, however, were not out on the streets; they were still very nervous of being recognised as friends of Jesus who, only seven weeks before, had been arrested and crucified; what if the authorities decided to take action against them too? So they kept a very low profile, but still met together behind closed doors to pray and keep alive their memories of Jesus and the amazing events in which they had been involved – especially since his death, for he had actually appeared to them several times, risen from the dead. But now, all that was over; he had said he was returning to God, but they were to wait in Jerusalem and God would fulfil his promise to them and give them power.

While pilgrims were enjoying the festival, these friends of Jesus were gathered together, probably in the same room where they had met with Jesus on the evening of his arrest when they had eaten the Passover supper together. Suddenly, strange things began to happen!

> Suddenly there was a noise from the sky which sounded like a strong wind blowing, and it filled the whole house where they were sitting. Then they saw what looked like tongues of fire which spread out and touched each person there. They were all filled with the Holy Spirit and began to talk in other languages, as the Spirit enabled them to speak. (Acts 2 vv. 2-4)

Almost before they knew what was happening, they were out among the crowds talking so excitedly that they were even accused by some of being drunk! Peter, however, now very bold, took the opportunity since the attention of the crowd was focused on them and spoke to them about Jesus. He created a tremendous impression, so great, in fact, that about three thousand people believed what he said about Jesus, and wanted to be baptised as a sign that they were now Christians.

The Celebrations

Whitsun is not observed as a festival to the same extent as Easter or Christmas, though in some communities it is a time when church people hold a 'procession of witness' through the streets. Adults and Sunday School children parade around the district and there is often a happy, almost carnival, air about it all.

When we asked about such a procession we were told, 'This occasion, according to the Acts of the Apostles, was one when the disciples became very bold and declared to everyone their message about Jesus; we feel we must do the same, not by preaching, but simply by letting people see that we also are disciples of Jesus in our time.'

Whitsun is also a time when some churches hold a service of confirmation in which young people or adults show their commitment to the Christian faith by becoming members of the Church. (See our other book, *Milestones*, for information about confirmation.)

Since Whitsun is especially a festival when the coming of the **Holy Spirit** with power on the early Christians is remembered, the church worship on that day usually focuses attention on this idea of the Holy Spirit.

One Christian's View of the Holy Spirit

We discussed this somewhat difficult idea of the Holy Spirit with a Christian Minister.

Our question: At Whitsun, you celebrate the coming of the Holy Spirit; does this mean that there was the sudden appearance of what we might describe as a 'new part' of God? Christians talk about God the Father, God the Son and God the Holy Spirit; should we think first of God the Father, then when Jesus came on the scene there were two of them, the Father and the Son, and at Pentecost there emerged a third, God the Holy Spirit?

Answer: No! Not at all! There are many references in the Old Testament to the Spirit of God, even as early as the Book of Genesis. I find it helpful to think of the Spirit as a way of describing God active in the world, though I must point out that not all Christians would agree with that point of view. What we are celebrating at Whitsun is the power of the Spirit beginning to show itself in the life of the early Church.

Our question: Can you help us to assist pupils in school understand more easily this rather difficult idea which is behind the festival of Whitsun?

Answer: I can at least try! I suggest that these pupils look around the classroom and imagine it on a dull, gloomy day; suddenly, the sun breaks through and the whole room is bright: you feel warmer and, somehow, you feel more alive! We cannot look at the sun, but when it shines we feel its warmth and absorb its life-giving energy and all that makes us feel good and we take a different view of life. I think the Holy Spirit is like that, better experienced than described. We cannot see the Holy Spirit, but we can feel something of his power. St Luke when writing about all this in the Acts of the Apostles had the same problem in attempting to describe the effect and the nature of the Holy Spirit on the early Christians.

Our question: Do you think Whitsun is an exciting Christian festival?

Answer: I could not honestly use the word 'exciting' to describe the way it is usually celebrated, but there is no doubt that the event we are remembering was one of the most exciting which has ever been experienced by the Church and it changed a group of rather frightened disciples of Jesus into men who were able boldly to proclaim his message.

Our question: Do you think it is rare for people today to experience the power of the Holy Spirit?

Answer: If you mean, do they experience the kind of things which happened to the early Christians on the Day of Pentecost, yes, that is rare. But I believe that Christians are experiencing the power of the Holy Spirit all the time. When Christians feel able, against the odds, to speak out for what they believe to be right and true, is that not the power of the Spirit helping them? When people face great difficulties, such as severe suffering or personal tragedy, but are helped by their faith to cope with the situation, is that not the power of the Holy Spirit helping them? Some might say, 'my faith in God' or 'my faith in Jesus helped me' but is that not the same thing? For I believe that the Holy Spirit is God active in and through the lives of people.

Task 1

(a) The event which is celebrated at Whitsun is described in the Acts of the Apostles chapter 2. Find this in a Bible and describe in your own words what happened (vv. 14-36 describe a sermon given by Peter on that occasion, but the rest of the chapter tells of the event and the people's reaction to it).

(b) What do you think was the most significant difference in the lives of the Apostles which was brought about by what is described as being 'filled with the Spirit'?

Task 2

During our interview with the Minister about Whitsun, he said he believed that 'the Holy Spirit is God active in and through the lives of people'. Choose someone, known to you, or, like Mother Teresa, an outstanding Christian, and show how it might be said that the power of the Holy Spirit is active through that person's life.

Muslim Festivals
Introduction

There are probably fewer festivals in Islam than in any other religion, and few of these are marked by dramatic celebrations such as exist in other faiths. They are, however, no less important than festivals in other faiths and are celebrated conscientiously and enthusiastically by Muslims all over the world.

An important difference between festivals in Islam and those of other faiths is that no Muslim festival is tied to any particular season of the year. It is, therefore, necessary to consider a few basic facts about the Muslim calendar.

The Muslim Calendar

Years
As far as years are concerned, Muslims consider that the occasion when the Prophet Muhammad moved from Mecca to Medina (see page 98) was so significant that they regard that year, 622 CE, as the year 1 AH (i.e. after Hijrah, the name given to his move to Medina). 1986 CE, therefore, in the Muslim calendar, is 1406 AH and that year began on 16th September 1985.

There is a simple formula to change from AH to CE and from CE to AH (the answers are approximate).

$$CE = \frac{32}{33} \times AH + 622$$

$$AH = (CE - 622) \times \frac{33}{32}$$

Months
The names of the months in the Muslim calendar are:

1	Muharram	7	Rajab
2	Safar	8	Sha'ban
3	Rabi ul-Awwal	9	Ramadan
4	Rabi ul-Akhir	10	Shawwal
or	Rabi ul-Thani	11	Dhu l-Qi'da
5	Jamada al-Awwal	12	Dhu l-Hijja
6	Jamada al-Akhir		
or	Jamada al-Thani		

The Muslim calendar, however, is based on phases of the moon, whereas the Western calendar is based on the time it takes for the earth to go round the sun. This means that there are 354 days in the Muslim calendar, but 365 days in the Western one with an extra day each fourth year. This difference means that Muslim festivals come ten or eleven days earlier each year in relation to the Western calendar, e.g. if Ramadan began in 1985 on 21st May, in 1986 it will begin on 10th May. Muslim festivals, therefore, will occur at some time in a cycle in all the seasons of the year. Each month in the Muslim calendar has either twenty-nine or thirty days; the month is said to begin with the sighting of the new moon.

Days
For Muslims, as for Jews, each new day begins in the evening and not at midnight; the first day of a festival, therefore, would begin at sunset and end at sunset on the following evening.

The Birthday of the Prophet

The 12th day of the month Rabi ul-Awwal is one of considerable importance in the Muslim calendar for this is the birthday of the Prophet Muhammad – Mawlid ul-Nabi. It is important to realise that Muslims do not worship Muhammad – they only worship Allah, the One God; they do, however, hold Muhammad in great honour, for they believe that he was the last of the prophets through whom Allah has revealed himself and his truth to man.

The Festival Story

It was the year 570 CE. In the city of Mecca, in the land we now know as Saudi Arabia, a child was born who was destined to become very great indeed.

Mecca was an important trading centre where there were many merchants. It was also a religious centre for the many Arab tribes. In Mecca there stood a cube-shaped building known as the **Kaaba**, which,

Procession on the Prophet's birthday

tradition said, had been there since the time of Abraham. At one corner of it there was a black stone; some say that it fell from Paradise when Adam disobeyed God; others say that the angel Gabriel presented Abraham with a white stone from Paradise but, because of the sins of man, that stone had become black.

No one would have imagined how great a person Muhammad was to become, for although he was born into a noble Arab tribe, he did not have the best of starts in life. His father, Abdullah, had died before he was born and Aminah, his mother, died when he was only six. When this happened, the six-year-old boy was looked after by his grandfather. Sadly, his grandfather only lived for another two years, so at the age of eight he was taken into the care of an uncle, Abu Talib, who was a merchant.

One story about Muhammad tells how, when he was twelve years old, he persuaded his uncle to allow him to accompany him on a business trip to Syria. As they arrived at the Syrian town of Busra, young Muhammad heard the sound of bells. He was told that these bells were calling Christian people to worship. Later he was to discover more about the Christians, for one of them, a Christian priest called Bahira, invited Abu Talib and young Muhammad to share a meal with him. It is said that Bahira invited them because he had experienced a vision in which he had seen the merchant's caravan approaching and felt sure that the boy accompanying the caravan was someone who was especially blessed by God and was destined for greatness.

Bahira told Abu Talib that he must take great care of his nephew for he had been chosen by God to be his special messenger.

It seems that young Muhammad was often troubled by the fact that, although Mecca, where he had grown up, was a religious centre, it was also a place where there was much selfishness and greed. Most of the Arabs of his day worshipped a variety of gods, represented by numerous idols. Many of these, in fact, were said to have been housed inside the Kaaba and people came there to worship, but their lives were no different: they were still selfish, greedy and did not care about their fellow men. All this seems to have made Muhammad think very deeply and helped to make him pursue a search for truth and meaning in life.

Celebration meal

The Celebrations

In the Mosque

The Birthday of the Prophet is an important occasion in the Muslim calendar. In our community there was a procession through the streets which finished up at the mosque, where, after worship, there was a celebration meal. Even the police who had assisted with the procession were invited to share in the meal! In the mosque, there is usually an address given to the worshippers present in which they are reminded of significant events in the life of the Prophet and of important developments in the history of their faith.

In the Home

The main celebration lies in the retelling of the many stories about Muhammad.

We visited the home of Mr and Mrs Ullah and asked their children if they would tell us some of their favourite stories which are retold in their family at this time. Here are some of the tales which they told us.

Wise Guidance

Once, the Kaaba was damaged by a flood and young Muhammad helped to rebuild it. All went well until the sacred black stone had to be replaced. A war nearly broke out over who should have the honour to replace it! Each of the chiefs claimed that he should have the honour; feelings were running very high indeed and tempers were becoming frayed when one old chief suggested that they should wait until the next morning and ask the first man who entered the Kaaba for his decision.

Next morning, the first man to enter was Muhammad. 'Here is Al Amin,' they cried, calling him by his nickname which meant 'the Trustworthy'. 'We will accept his guidance!' Muhammad asked for a sheet to be brought; he laid it on the ground and placed the black stone in the middle of it. He then told the chiefs of each tribe to take hold of the sheet and slowly raise it to the height where the stone was to be built in. Gently it was slid into place from the sheet; everyone was satisfied for they had all had a share in the honour. Muhammad's wise decision had avoided strife between the tribes.

Muhammad, Friend of Animals

The message proclaimed by the Prophet was that there is only One God and that it is his will that men should serve him and be kind to one another, especially to orphans, widows and animals.

One day when he went into his house, he saw his cat sleeping with her kittens on the cloak which he wanted to wear. He felt it would be unkind to disturb it, so he cut off the end of the cloak on which the sleeping cat lay and wrapped what remained around his own shoulders!

On another occasion he was walking along one of the narrow streets of his town when a camel suddenly appeared, running towards him. People were very afraid and were rushing to hide from its large hooves and strong teeth. Muhammad was used to these animals, for at one time he had been a camel driver, so he easily stopped the animal. The breathless owner came to him and thanked him for his help, then turned to give the animal a beating.

'Why don't you feed the animal properly?' asked the Prophet. 'He is complaining that he is hungry. He would not run away if you treated him well.' The man was rather shocked but admitted that he had been wrong. The camel was not there only to be his servant; it was also an animal which deserved to be cared for.

Hatred Overcome by Kindness

After Muhammad began to proclaim the message Allah had given him, there were many people who disliked him. They did not agree with his criticism of idol worship and when he told them that Allah wanted them to be good and generous, they did not want to listen for they found it easier to be greedy and selfish.

One woman who did not like Muhammad used to sweep her dust and rubbish over him as he passed her house on his way to pray. The Prophet always turned his head and, smiling, greeted her as he would a friend, 'Assalam o Alaikum!' The woman never replied; she just swept more dust over him!

One day, as Muhammad came near the woman's house, no dust or rubbish came his way! The woman was nowhere to be seen. The Prophet asked the neighbours about her; they were surprised at his interest for they knew how she had treated him. They told him that she lived alone and was very ill. At once, Muhammad went to her house where he set to work cooking a meal, fetching water from the well and sweeping away the dust and rubbish. The woman was amazed to see someone helping her and more so when she realised who he was! She was sorry for her bad deeds and in time became a good Muslim following his example of kindness and truthfulness.

Task 1

Using the information gained from the stories told in this chapter, write a description of the kind of person you consider Muhammad must have been.

Task 2

Stories such as these convey important aspects of Muslim teaching about how people ought to live. Take each of the stories in turn and state what the teaching is that it presents.

Do you agree that such teaching encourages a better way of life? Give reasons for your answer.

Task 3

During the procession in our community to mark the Prophet's Birthday, as they walked, the Muslims shouted the opening words of the Call to Prayer, in Arabic, 'Allah is the greatest!'

(a) Why do you think they were not shouting 'Muhammad is the greatest!'?

(b) What does such a procession say about their beliefs and their faith?

Task 4

Study carefully the photographs in this chapter. What conclusions do you reach about the Muslims in this community? Consider especially what the photograph showing the celebration meal tells us.

Ramadan and Eid ul-Fitr

A very important month in the Muslim year is the month known as **Ramadan**. Perhaps we should not think of Ramadan so much as a time of festival but rather as a time of most important religious observance, for on every day of the month of Ramadan, Muslims do not eat or drink during the hours of daylight. This period of fasting ends when the next new moon appears, for that marks the beginning of the month of Shawwal. The first day of that month is held as a joyous festival known as **Eid ul-Fitr**, or 'the Fast-breaking Festival'.

The Festival Story

The Prophet Muhammad became known in Mecca as Al Amin, the Trustworthy, for he became a dependable merchant. A wealthy widow, Khadijah, heard of his sound reputation and offered him the job of managing her trading caravans. Muhammad accepted and travelled far and wide trading with people in distant lands and cities. He journeyed to such places as Jerusalem, Damascus and Syria and, in the course of his business, came to know many Jews and Christians and learned a great deal about both these faiths. Khadijah always eagerly awaited Muhammad's return to Mecca and, eventually, although she was considerably older than Muhammad, they married and were very happy together.

At the age of forty, Muhammad seemed to have everything a man could desire: he had wealth, a good wife and four daughters. It seemed that the only real misfortune he had suffered since his marriage was the death of his son. He was, however, very dissatisfied and felt sure that life must hold considerably more than wealth and a successful career; he longed to find a deeper meaning in his existence. It was with such thoughts in his head that he regularly left Mecca and went off to the hills of Hira where he could be alone to fast and meditate.

During the month of Ramadan, Muhammad finally found his answer. Towards the end of the month, he had again climbed the mountains of Hira, entered a cave and spent the day in fasting and the night in prayer. Just before dawn he saw what he afterwards described as an angel holding out an embroidered scroll. He was commanded to read the words written on the scroll; Muhammad hesitated because he could not read. Three times the command was given, 'Read!' and three times Muhammad felt himself gripped by a strange, powerful force as the word was spoken.

Finally, reciting after the angel, Muhammad said, 'In the name of thy Lord who created man from a drop of blood: read in the name of the almighty Allah who taught man the use of the pen and taught him what he knew not before. . .'

Muhammad repeated these words until he was able to say them perfectly and then the angel disappeared and he found himself alone in the dark cave. He was alone, and yet he still felt the strange force which had surrounded him during the vision. He felt afraid for he did not understand what had happened to him.

He began to make his way home, stumbling down the mountain path in fear, when he heard the voice again. This time the vision of the angel seemed to fill the whole sky and the voice said, 'O Muhammad! Truly thou art the messenger of Allah and I am his angel, Gabriel!'

The Prophet hurried home to tell Khadijah of his extraordinary experience. His wife had no doubt that he had been called to be Allah's messenger, but Muhammad was afraid that he might have been influenced by some evil spirit, so they consulted a wise and respected relation, Waraqa. This old man said he was sure that this was indeed a revelation from the same angel who had appeared to Abraham and to Moses.

Months passed and Muhammad had no further revelations until one night he was awakened from sleep to hear the same voice as before, saying, 'O thou wrapped in a mantle! Arise! Deliver thy warning and magnify the Lord!'

Muhammad had many other revelations after this and he memorised all that he was told. He passed on these messages to those who were prepared to follow him and they wrote down all that he recited to them. Years later, all of these sayings were gathered together and written in one book, the Holy **Qur'an**.

This Qur'an contained a new message and a new way of life which Muhammad had to teach to the people. Such a task was not to be easy in a city like Mecca in which there was a great deal of idol worship, for the essence of the message was that there is only one God, Allah, and he alone must be worshipped. The people must turn from their idolatry and other evil practices and follow the way to salvation shown by the Prophet.

Prayers in the mosque

The Imam addresses the men

The Celebrations

The Holy Qur'an commands Muslims to fast for the hours of daylight during the whole month of Ramadan. Every Muslim over the age of twelve who is physically fit is expected to observe the fast.

Each day the fast begins when the first sign of daylight is observed on the horizon and it continues until darkness falls. You will remember that the Muslim calendar is worked out according to phases of the moon and not the sun, so the Muslim year is slightly shorter than the year as we know it in the West. This means that Ramadan comes at a different time in our calendar each year. Obviously, therefore, the length of the fast each day will depend on whether Ramadan falls in winter or summer and also on where you are in the world.

We asked Mr Ullah, a Muslim who lives

in our community, if he would tell us about his daily routine during the month of Ramadan.

'Every day during Ramadan,' he told us, 'I rise very early and eat a meal before dawn. We call this meal **suhoor** and it is important that it should be eaten. After the meal I express aloud my intention to observe the fast during the day and I follow this with the dawn prayers. As you know, Muslims pray at five set times each day all through the year.

'I am a shopkeeper, and although it is Ramadan, I open my business at the usual time and only leave the shop to observe the usual times of prayer. During Ramadan, I make a special effort every evening to go to the mosque. Normally I only go for the Friday prayers and service but I find it particularly helpful to share the company of fellow Muslims at worship during the fast.

'Many of my fellow Muslims feel the same and there is usually a good number of worshippers present. Before prayers we go through the usual ritual of washing our hands and arms up to the elbows, our feet, our mouths and nostrils. We know when it is time for the prayers to start because one of our number stands in the room set aside for prayer and makes the call to prayer. Of course, if we were in a Muslim country that prayer call would be sounding out from the minaret and would be heard all over the community.

'We follow the Imam, the leader in our mosque, in the various positions we adopt for our prayers, thinking about the words which accompany each movement. Each complete set of movements is called a **rakat**; during these prayers we make four rakats. Our prayers end with **du'a**: these are our personal, individual prayers in which we raise our hands to Allah and pray for our relatives, ourselves, or for any matter which is particularly on our minds.

'The Imam gives a short talk which lasts until the sun has set; it is then time for what we call **iftar**, the breaking of the fast. Food is set out in the mosque and we sit on the floor and receive some of the light foods, a glass of water and some fruit; it is a custom to break the fast with some dates, but, before eating, each of us thanks Allah for helping us keep the fast.

'Before leaving the mosque it is time for prayer again; this is the fourth prayer time of the day. After observing that, I go home for the evening meal which my wife has prepared. She has followed our custom of praying at home; it is usually only the men who pray at the mosque.

'My final visit to the mosque for the day is for the night prayers, which, during Ramadan, is followed by a reading from the Holy Qur'an. You will have realised from what I have told you that during Ramadan, especially, there is an emphasis on prayer as well as fasting, and one feels very close to Allah. It is important for us to read the Qur'an particularly at this time and remember that it was during this month in our calendar that the word of Allah was first given to us through the holy Prophet Muhammad. I aim to read a part of the Qur'an each day, so that by the end of Ramadan I have read it completely.'

Ihtekaf

During the last ten days of Ramadan, some Muslims choose to devote their complete attention to Allah's revelation in the Qur'an. In the mosque, special arrangements are made for them to be alone, just as Muhammad was alone in the cave at Hira. Part of the mosque is made especially private so that any man who wishes to study the Qur'an and pray, may do so. Those who have chosen to do this only join the rest of their fellow Muslims for the prayer times and to break the fast; the rest of the time, they remain alone. This practice is known as **ihtekaf** and those who observe it, as you can imagine, feel very close to Allah.

Iftar

Lailat ul-Qadr

During Ramadan there is one special night known as Lailat ul-Qadr, 'the Night of Power'. This is the night on which the Prophet Muhammad had his vision and the beginnings of the Holy Qur'an were revealed to him. Muslims say that they do not know exactly which night this was, but it was probably one of the last ten nights of Ramadan. Most Muslims observe the night of the 27th of Ramadan as Lailat ul-Qadr.

Muslims are told that they should try to stay awake during the whole night, reading the Qur'an, offering special prayers and asking forgiveness from Allah. In our community, many Muslims who were not able to spend the last ten days of Ramadan at the mosque, nevertheless did spend the whole night of the 27th at the mosque. Mr Ullah described it as 'an experience which made me feel especially near to Allah, even more so than on any other occasion.'

One Muslim tradition says:

> When Lailat ul-Qadr comes, Allah commands Gabriel to descend with seventy thousand angels. With them are torches of light and they set them up in the mosque at Mecca, in the Sanctuary at Medina and in Jerusalem. Gabriel sets up his torch on the very roof of the Kaaba. Then the angels separate over the lands of the earth and visit every Muslim whom they find at prayer and worship: they salute him and clasp his hand and say, 'Amen', to his petition and ask forgiveness for all Muslims and pray for them till daybreak.

Eid ul-Fitr

It is understandable that Muslims welcome the first day of the month Shawwal, for that is the day of the Fast-breaking Festival, Eid ul-Fitr. The fasting of Ramadan is over for another year. We must not think, however, that the Eid is just an

Collecting on Eid ul-Fitr

excuse for over-eating, to make up for the lack of food during Ramadan! It is very much a religious festival. The day begins with prayers, usually at the mosque, and there is usually a sermon given by the Imam. In the sermon given at the mosque in our community, the Imam followed the custom of reminding the worshippers of their duty to care for those who are in need. A collection was made in a sheet and, as you can see from the photograph, the amount given was quite substantial! This money would be used in a variety of ways to assist Muslims who were in need of help.

The mosque was crowded for the Eid worship and all the people were attractively dressed in new clothes, for just as fasting is a duty to be observed during

'Eid mubarak!'

Ramadan, so also it is a duty to celebrate joyfully the festival.

After the worship, all present remained to talk and to embrace each other with the greeting, 'Eid mubarak!' which means, 'a happy and blessed festival!'

The Eid at Home

At Mr Ullah's home, special foods had been prepared for the family celebration. The children received gifts from family and friends, and there were many greetings cards on display. Many of these had come from Pakistan where the Ullah family had friends and relations. There was a very happy atmosphere as the family enjoyed the festivities of the Eid. The children had followed the custom of painting designs on their hands as part of the Eid celebration and were proud to show us what they had done.

Later in the day, the family went to visit the cemetery where some of their relatives were buried. The Eid is a time also to remember friends and relatives who have died. At the grave, Mr and Mrs Ullah said a prayer in which they were giving thanks for the memory of their loved ones who were dead. Eid ul-Fitr is very much a family time, when the unity of the family both those present and those who are dead is emphasised.

Interview with Mr Ullah

We took the opportunity on this occasion to put some questions to Mr Ullah about Ramadan and Eid ul-Fitr.

Our question: What do you see as the importance of fasting?

Answer: Observing the fast helps us to develop self-control. The discipline of it helps us to overcome selfishness and greed. It is rather like retraining ourselves each year to carry out our duties to Allah and to our fellow men. In addition we learn each year what it is like to be hungry and it is a regular reminder of the fact that we should care about our fellow men in some places of the world who are always hungry.

I could eat during Ramadan and no one would know; I could pretend to be observing the fast but privately eat a snack now and again to keep me from feeling too hungry! But Allah would know, and I would know myself that I had not been true to my duty and my belief as a Muslim.

Our question: Do you find the month of Ramadan very difficult?

Answer: I will not pretend that it is easy; it is difficult, and yet that is what makes it so worthwhile. It presents a challenge to us and it is good to face up to such a challenge. The Holy Qur'an teaches us that the purpose of the fast is not to make us suffer, but to develop in us self-restraint and obedience to the will of Allah.

Our question: We were impresed with the happy and joyous atmosphere on the day

of Eid ul-Fitr. Can you explain briefly for us what exactly Muslims are celebrating?

Answer: Yes, it is a very happy day, not just because the fast is over and we have faced the challenge it presented. We are thanking Allah for his gift of the Holy Qur'an which guides us in life. We are also thanking him for the strength to observe Ramadan and for the great sense of unity we feel with our fellow Muslims. We are especially full of joy that we have been obedient to the will of Allah. We are actually forbidden to fast on Eid ul-Fitr, so we believe that Allah has decreed that this is to be a happy day.

Task 1

At Ramadan, Muslims think of the origins of the Qur'an. Write a paragraph to say why a Muslim would object to Muhammad being described as 'the author' of the Qur'an.

Task 2

Imagine you are a Muslim living in Britain. Write an account of a typical day in your life during the month of Ramadan. Remember to include the times of your prayers; also describe how you feel at different times of the day about your fast. Include a few sentences stating what you believe is the purpose and the benefit of your fasting.

Task 3

In the photograph you can see Mr Ullah's daughter holding out her hand which she has decorated. Why do you think she has marked her hand with the half moon and the star? Draw *either* an appropriate Muslim design to decorate a hand *or* design a greetings card for Eid ul-Fitr.

Task 4

What similarities and what differences do you recognise between the celebration of Eid ul-Fitr and any happy festival in another faith which you know about?

Hijrah

New Year's Day for the Muslim is the first day of the month Muharram. This day is not merely the first of a new year but is also the anniversary of a very important stage in the development of Islam. It marks the occasion when Muhammad left Mecca in the year 622 CE to settle in Medina.

The Festival Story

In the chapter about Ramadan and Eid ul-Fitr, you read the story of how the Prophet Muhammad, through his visions, was given the messages from Allah which later were to be written down in the Holy Qur'an. Muhammad found that when he tried to proclaim his message to the people of Mecca, he met with great opposition and made many enemies. After all, if he was saying that they should not love money and should share what they had with those in need, such a message would not appeal to the wealthy Meccan merchants! In addition, his message that there is only one God would be disturbing to those who were used to the worship of various idols.

The words 'Islam' and 'Muslim' both come from the same Arabic word which means 'to submit'. Muhammad's message was essentially that the people should submit to Allah and honour him as the One God. There were many in Mecca who had no intention of submitting to this God. There were, however, visitors to Mecca who heard Muhammad's message and became believers. Among them were six men who came from Yathrib, a town some 300 miles north-east of Mecca. These men shared their new-found faith with others when they returned home and so the number of converts and supporters of Muhammad in Yathrib grew to be considerably more than those in Mecca. Muhammad was invited to join them and leave Mecca where it was becoming increasingly dangerous because of his enemies.

Migration to Medina (Yathrib)

In the year 619 two of Muhammad's strongest supporters, his uncle Abu Talib and his wife Khadijah, both died. During the next three years, the opposition in Mecca increased and there were plans to kill Muhammad, so one night in the year 622, he and Abu Bakr, his loyal friend, left the city, managing to avoid those who had been watching them for an opportunity to take the Prophet's life. They took refuge in a cave when they realised that they were being pursued. After they were inside the cave, a spider fortunately spun a web which covered the entrance; also it is said that a dove built a nest on a branch which lay across the entrance and laid eggs in it, so when their enemies arrived, they were convinced that there could be no one in that cave and so began to look elsewhere. Muhammad and Abu Bakr stayed in the cave for three days before daring to attempt the remainder of their journey to Yathrib.

The Prophet was welcome in Yathrib and gradually the number of his followers increased as more and more acted on his teaching and were willing to submit to Allah; so Yathrib became a Muslim city. It was renamed Madinat ul-Nabi, 'the city of the Prophet', a name which has been shortened simply to Medina.

Prayer Call Introduced

Muhammad taught that there should be prayer to Allah five times every day. There was some discussion in Medina about how the people could be called together for their prayers. In the end, Muhammad decided that the most effective way was for someone to shout aloud words which summed up the faith and way of life of the Muslim. It was a freed negro slave, Bilal, who was the first to be taught these words by Muhammad, and it is said that his melodious voice echoed across the city of Medina calling the faithful to prayer. This call to prayer is known as the **Adhan** and the Arabic words still echo out five times a day wherever there is a mosque:

> God is the greatest [four times]
> I bear witness that there is no God but Allah [twice]
> I bear witness that Muhammad is the messenger of Allah [twice]
> Come to prayer [twice]
> Come to security [twice]
> God is the greatest [twice]
> There is no God but Allah.

Return to Mecca

During the next few years following Muhammad's arrival in Medina, the Meccans sent bands of armed men to attack the city, for they felt threatened by the success of Muhammad's teaching. However, these attacks were unsuccessful for Muhammad's growing number of followers were also prepared to take up arms in his defence. In the year 630 they were strong enough to go on the offensive: they attacked Mecca and easily took control. The Kaaba, the cube-shaped building in Mecca which had for long been regarded as a holy place, was now cleansed of all the influence of pagan worship; the idols of various gods which had been kept inside were removed and destroyed and the interior of the building left empty as a symbol that this is a house for Allah alone; he is the only God. It is to this building that all Muslims turn for their prayers, wherever they are in the world.

Muhammad's flight from Mecca to Medina turned out to be so important a stage in the growth of Islam that the Muslim calendar dates from that event. The year 622 CE is, for the Muslim, the year 1 AH; **Hijrah** is the name Muslims give to Muhammad's move from Mecca to Medina, so AH means 'after Hijrah'. 1986 in the Western calendar, therefore, is the year 1406 in the Muslim calendar.

Call to prayer

The Celebrations

The Day of Hijrah, like the Birthday of the Prophet, is not marked by dramatic ceremonies; we were assured, however, that this does not mean it is unimportant. It is a day for Muslims to attend the mosque for special acts of worship, in which prayers are offered and an address is given by the Imam. It is a time when the stories of Muhammad are recalled, especially those about his migration from Mecca to Medina.

In the mosque in our community, the Imam chose to remind the worshippers of the way in which the stories of Hijrah emphasise the guidance which Allah gave in all these important events.

Allah's Protection in the Cave

The Imam reminded his people of the story of Muhammad and Abu Bakr taking refuge in the cave to evade their pursuers from Mecca.

'They were exhausted,' he said, 'and as Abu Bakr sank down inside the cave, he gasped, "May Allah protect us!" "Take courage," replied Muhammad, "Allah will hear you." Suddenly, they heard the sound of the enemy approaching; Abu Bakr was trembling as he said, "What can we do? There are obviously many of them and there are only two of us!" Muhammad replied, "You are mistaken; there are three of us, for Allah is with us!"

'They heard the voices and were astonished to hear it said that they could not possibly be hiding in that cave. "Look," said the voice, "the entrance is covered by a spider's web and there is a dove nesting in the branches overhanging the path!" The troop of horsemen moved off to look elsewhere for the Prophet. Clearly, Allah was with them protecting and guiding their lives.'

Building a Mosque in Medina

'Remember,' continued the Imam, 'how Allah is said to have guided Muhammad about where he should live and worship in Medina. There were many who pleaded for the honour of giving him hospitality; politely, however, he refused them all, saying that wherever his camel rested, here he would make his home and here would be set up a place of worship. The camel eventually fell to its knees on a plot of ground by the house of one Abu Ayyub Ansari. Here, before long, the foundations were laid for the first mosque in Medina. While it was being built, the Prophet proclaimed his message in the open air; he also worked hard himself, along with his followers, in the exhausting task of building. Once again, Allah showed his guidance, even in such a matter as where the first mosque should be built.'

The Imam urged his fellow Muslims to have faith in the goodness of Allah; just as he guided and protected the Prophet at the time of the Hijrah, so on this Day of Hijrah, and in the days and years ahead, he will guide and protect the faithful who trust him and submit their lives to him.

Task 1
'It seems strange to celebrate Muhammad's flight to Medina. It would be more appropriate to celebrate his return to Mecca in 630 CE.' Imagine you are a Muslim replying to such a statement; how would you explain the celebration of Hijrah?

Task 2
One of the ninety-nine titles which Muslims have for Allah is 'the Guide'. What is there in the stories relating to Hijrah which emphasises a strong Muslim belief in Allah as the one who guides?

Task 3
What are the advantages for Muslims of their being called to prayer by the words of the Adhan, rather than by the ringing of bells or some other method?

Eid ul-Adha

The twelfth month of the Muslim calendar is Dhu l-Hijja, the month of Pilgrimage. Every Muslim is expected at least once in a lifetime to make a pilgrimage to Mecca; the pilgrimage is known as **Hajj** and is carried out from the 8th to the 13th of Dhu l-Hijja. During this time various rituals are carried out by the pilgrims both in Mecca and in other holy places nearby. One of these places is Mina which is about eight kilometres from Mecca; one of the rituals performed here is the sacrifice of animals on the 10th of Dhu l-Hijja. This part of the Hajj in fact marks the beginning of a major Muslim festival which is celebrated by Muslims all over the world, whether they have made the journey to Mecca or not; the festival is known as Eid ul-Adha, 'the Festival of Sacrifice'.

Eid ul-Adha at the mosque

The Festival Story

The main event being celebrated at Eid ul-Adha is the Prophet Abraham's willingness to sacrifice his son, Ishmael, to Allah. Jews look back to Abraham as their great ancestor and he is sometimes referred to as 'the Father of the Hebrew people'. Muslims also, however, regard him as their great ancestor; while the Jewish people trace their ancestry back to Abraham through his son, Isaac, Muslims trace the ancestry of the Arab peoples to him through his son Ishmael.

The story which is the background to Eid ul-Adha is essentially the story of Abraham which is related in the Book of Genesis in the Old Testament, with one very significant difference. Whereas in the Old Testament version it is his son Isaac that Abraham attempts to sacrifice, in the Muslim tradition it is Ishmael.

According to the Qur'an, Abraham met with opposition because of his criticism of idol worship; his response was, 'I will take refuge with my Lord; He will guide me. Grant me a son, Lord, and let him be a righteous man.'

His prayers were answered and when his son was old enough to work with his father, Abraham said to him, 'My son, I dreamt that I was sacrificing you. Tell me what you think.' He replied, 'Father, do as you are bidden. Allah willing, you shall find me faithful.' When they had both submitted to Allah's will, and Abraham had laid his son down, ready to take his life, Allah spoke to him, saying, 'Abraham, you have fulfilled your vision'; the Qur'an concludes this account by saying, 'and Allah bestowed on him the praise of later generations: Peace be on Abraham!'

Some Muslim traditions say that Abraham blindfolded his son and prepared to cut his throat. He shut his eyes as he made the cut, but when he opened them, his son was safe and well; the angel Gabriel had performed a miracle and replaced Ishmael with a ram. Others say that Satan tempted Ishmael to run away, and Abraham to give up the idea of sacrificing his own son; each time, however, they resisted the temptation. Allah was impressed by this show of faith and provided a ram to be sacrificed instead of Ishmael.

The Celebrations

On the Hajj

If you were a Muslim following the pilgrimage you would be at Mina, near Mecca, on the 10th day of Dhu l-Hijja. On the previous evening, you would have collected forty-nine pebbles to use in a ceremony which immediately precedes Eid ul-Adha. In Mina are three stone pillars which are said to mark the spot where Ishmael was tempted by the devil to disobey his father Abraham. This relates to the tradition which says that Ishmael resisted the temptation by throwing stones at him.

The pilgrims crowd round these stone pillars and throw the pebbles which they have collected as hard as they can at the pillars. This act is a forceful reminder to them that they also face temptation in their lives and they want to oppose all evil and do the will of Allah.

This action leads into the celebration of Eid ul-Adha which ends the pilgrimage. For the pilgrim, the main aspect of the festival is the offering of a sacrifice: usually a lamb, a sheep or a goat. Bedouin tribesmen lead large herds of animals into the area to be sold to the pilgrims; many of the pilgrims then slaughter the animal they have purchased, in the way acceptable to Muslims, by slitting its throat. A share of the meat must, according to the Qur'an, be given to the poor; now, because of the large quantities involved, a refrigerated store has been built at Mina so that meat which cannot be distributed to the poor

The Imam's talk to the congregation

the courtyard outside the mosque.

During the service, the Imam gave a talk. In the course of it he reminded the worshippers that this is the festival of sacrifice.

'Our thoughts go back,' he said, 'to the Prophet Abraham's willingness to sacrifice his son as an offering to Allah, so great was his desire to honour and serve Allah.

'Our thoughts go also to our brothers who are making the Hajj and who, at this time, like us, are worshipping and will be offering their sacrifices to Allah. I would remind you, brothers, that the spirit of Hajj is the spirit of total sacrifice; those who are making the Hajj have not just made the sacrifice of an animal; they have given up personal comfort to make the journey; they have given up money, and the companionship of family and friends; they have sacrificed their normal dress to put on the pilgrim's dress, common to all making the Hajj, and thus have sacrificed their status in life, their nationality, and everything which may have been a matter of pride; all has been sacrificed in the interests of equality with all brother Muslims.

'I urge you, my brothers, as later today you also make your sacrifices of animals, to make these symbols of your willingness to be devoted to the service of Allah.'

straight away can be given later.

In our Community
Eid ul-Adha is not just for those making the pilgrimage; Muslims throughout the world turn their thoughts to the pilgrims and also observe special ceremonies within their own communities.

At the Mosque
The day began for Muslims in our community with a service at the mosque. There were so many worshippers present for this festival worship that there was not room for all inside the mosque so, as you can see in the photograph on page 101, prayers were offered by many of them in

Sacrifices
All the Muslim families who could afford it had made plans for the sacrifice of an animal. Special arrangements had been made with the authorities at the local abattoir so that the animals could be slaughtered in a way acceptable to Muslim law. Some families had got together and purchased a cow; others had simply bought a lamb; the men were present at the abattoir and offered prayers as their particular animal was killed.

Two thirds of each animal was given away, usually to families who were in need and were perhaps too poor to make a

103

Celebration meal

sacrifice for themselves. The remainder was cooked for the festival meal when the family shared in the joyous aspects of the Eid.

There were some families who, instead of sacrificing an animal themselves, sent money to relatives or friends abroad; most of the Muslim families in our community had originated in Pakistan, so many were making the Eid sacrifice by making sure that poorer families in Pakistan were able to celebrate the Eid and share in a festival meal.

The Celebration Meal
The children especially looked forward to the festival meal! The women of the families had been busy after their prayers preparing the meal. It was a happy occasion as many families were reunited and as friends called to wish them 'Eid mubarak!',

'a happy festival!' They had also received many cards from friends both at home and abroad which brought similar good wishes.

Before beginning the meal, prayers were said, and so the festival of sacrifice continued as they enjoyed the meal together.

Questions about the Festival

After the meal, we questioned Mr Khan, one of our Muslim friends, about this festival.
Our question: We know that Eid ul-Adha means 'the Festival of Sacrifice'; can you tell us more about this idea of sacrifice? We tend to think of the word in two ways sacrifice can mean the killing of an animal in a ritual way as an offering, or, more

104

often, it means giving something up, denying ourselves something, which we really wanted.

Answer: Muslims also think of sacrifice in that way. The sacrifice of the animal is really a symbol of our willingness to offer much more to Allah. Granted, we eat some of the meat of the animal, but, by giving away most of it, we are making a sacrifice in that other sense of the word.

Our question: Does this need for sacrifice in both senses of the word make Islam a hard faith to follow? Are you saying that to be a Muslim, you are always having to deny yourself many things you really want?

Answer: I do not see it like that at all. Certainly it does not mean that we live a miserable existence! You have seen us celebrating the Eid and I am sure you did not think we were miserable! You see, life for everyone is full of sacrifices. When my wife and I wanted the joy of having children, we had to be prepared to give up some of our freedom, and again, we did so willingly. So in our religion, we give up time, which we could use for other activities, to pray, but we receive the blessing of Allah when we pray; we give up money and time to make the Hajj, but our lives are enriched by the contact with the holy places and with the fellowship of so many other fellow Muslims. We gave up money to buy an animal for sacrifice, but we have the satisfaction of knowing that we have helped others less fortunate, for we have shared it with them, and we have the pleasure of knowing that we have been obedient to Allah. Where, I ask you, is the hardship of making such sacrifices in our lives? All of these are worthwhile to us because we know we have done Allah's will!

Task 1
What reasons might Abraham have had for thinking he should offer his son as a sacrifice to Allah? What religious lesson can you draw from this story?

Task 2
What value, if any, do you see in such an action as throwing pebbles at stone pillars and remembering Abraham and Ishmael resisting temptation? Give reasons for your answer.

Task 3
(a) Summarise in your own words Mr Khan's views about sacrifice. Do you agree with him? Give reasons for your answer.

(b) What sacrifices have you made? Were they worthwhile?

(c) Think of one religion you have studied in which there is no animal sacrifice; how do you think that religion, nevertheless, demands sacrifice from those who follow it?

'Eid mubarak!'

105

Sikh Festivals
Introduction

The Sikh faith is, of course, an Indian religion; it began in the fifteenth century as a result of the teaching of Guru Nanak who lived in the Punjab in north-west India. Although this faith grew up against a background of Hinduism, the Sikhs developed their own customs and practices. As time went on, even if they were observing a Hindu festival, they did not do so according to Hindu custom but observed it in a way which was in line with their own beliefs.

As events occurred which proved to be significant to Sikhs, they came to believe that these should be remembered and celebrated annually and so a pattern for Sikh festivals gradually evolved.

The Sikh emblem

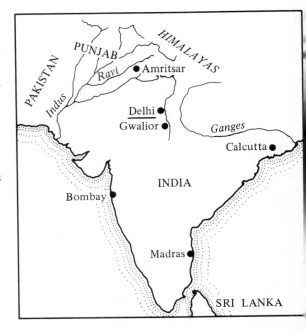

The Sikh Calendar

Since the Sikh faith is an Indian religion the months of their calendar are the same as those in Hinduism (for the names of these months see page 7). This means that Sikh festivals, like Hindu ones, do not always come on the same date in relation to the Western calendar, though, like Hindu festivals, they always belong to the same season of the year. There is, however, one festival which is different: that is the festival of **Baisakhi** which is always on the 13th April, except that every 36th year it is on the 14th April.

Baisakhi

Baisakhi is probably the most important of the Sikh festivals for it celebrates the beginning of the **Khalsa**, the Sikh brotherhood. It is also a new year festival, for it marks the beginning of the Sikh religious year.

Baisakhi was originally a Hindu spring festival in northern India, but the third Sikh Guru, Amar Das, decided that Sikhs should separate themselves from Hindu celebrations and mark this day in their own way, so he ordered the Sikhs to assemble before him for worship every Baisakhi. Amar Das was, in this way, asking the Sikhs to make up their minds where they stood as far as their faith was concerned. The tenth Guru, Gobind, called on the Sikhs to make an even more difficult decision on Baisakhi day in the year 1699; it is this event which has made this the important and distinctive festival for Sikhs everywhere.

The Festival Story

In the year 1699 Guru Gobind summoned the Sikhs to gather at Anandpur in the Punjab to celebrate Baisakhi. He was anxious to have as many as possible present, for it was a difficult time for Sikhs: many were being persecuted and were tempted to give up their faith. As a result of the Guru's summons, thousands gathered around a tent which had been erected and waited for the Guru to address them.

Guru Gobind emerged from the tent and, to everyone's surprise, he was fully armed; he stood on a platform where all could see him and, instead of words of blessing which they expected to hear, the assembled company listened to a very strange request: 'Who is willing to give his head as a proof of his faith?' There was a hush in the shocked crowd until one man, Daya Ram, came forward and the Guru took him into the tent. After a few minutes, Guru Gobind re-emerged holding his sword on which blood stains were clearly visible!

The Guru continued with his awful request until, in all, five men had gone into the tent to give their lives for their faith. When Guru Gobind went into the tent with the fifth man, Himmab Rai, he remained there for a long time; when he did come out, there was a gasp of relief from the crowd, for following him were the five volunteers! They were all now dressed like the Guru, carrying swords and all perfectly well!

The Guru called the five brave men his **Panj Pyares** and declared them to be the foundation of the Sikh brotherhood which he called the Khalsa, which means, 'the Pure Ones'. He then baptised his five 'Pure Ones' by giving them a mixture, which was to be known as **Amrit**, to drink; he also sprinkled some of it on their heads and their eyes.

This baptism introduced by Guru Gobind created a community of united, righteous men who would fight for justice and freedom against those who would oppress them and take away the liberties of others. The Amrit ceremony was to become the ceremony of initiation into the Khalsa; today any Sikh man or woman who wishes to be committed fully to the Sikh faith will undergo such a ceremony. (For information on the Amrit ceremony, and a longer account of the Festival story, see pages 63-7 in our book, *Milestones*.)

The Celebrations

In our community in 1984 the celebration of Baisakhi was actually divided between two days because in that year April 13th was a Friday which was, of course, a working day. Certain rites were carried out on the 13th but the Baisakhi worship was observed on the following Sunday. This was to allow as many as possible to celebrate the festival.

The Thirteenth of April
Although the 13th was a normal working day, many Sikhs rose early and made their way to the gurdwara to witness the beginning of a continuous reading from the **Guru Granth Sahib**. This continuous reading from the holy book is known as **Akhand Path** and always takes place on such special occasions, as is mentioned in the section on Gurpurbs on page 124. After opening prayers, **Karah Parshad**, the Sikhs' holy food, was given to all the worshippers and then the reading began. The reading would continue with different readers following each other until the whole of the Guru Granth Sahib had been read by Sunday morning.

Once the reading was in progress, the Sangat, i.e. the congregation, moved outside the gurdwara for the highlight of the morning's celebrations. A Sikh gurdwara can be easily distinguished by the **Nishan Sahib**, the Sikh flag, which marks it out as a place of worship for Sikhs. The flag which bears the Sikh emblem is usually flying on a tall flagpole which has some decorative material wrapped around it. If you look carefully at the photograph on page 109, and on page 106, you will see that the emblem consists of a central, double-edged sword called a **Khanda**;

Reading the Guru Granth Sahib

The Nishan Sahib

Guru Gobind Singh used such a sword to stir the Amrit on that historic occasion in 1699 which is remembered in the festival story. One edge symbolises God's power and justice, the other, freedom and authority given to the man who obeys God. On the outside of the Khanda, in the emblem, are two curved swords symbolising religious and political freedom; it was for this cause that Guru Gobind founded the Khalsa. Surrounding the Khanda is the **Chakra**, a circle symbolic of the unity of the Sikhs and their belief in one God 'whose name is truth'.

This emblem on the flag is clearly very important to Sikhs and, at the beginning of a new religious year, the flagpole is washed, re-covered in the decorative material and a new flag hoisted. In this way, Sikhs show their loyalty to everything the flag symbolises and rededicate themselves to their faith.

The ceremony was conducted with great reverence and, while the flagpole was being lowered, the congregation sang hymns to the accompaniment of the harmonium and drum. Once lowered, the pole was placed on tables set out to receive it and the strips of material were removed. Some water and yoghurt were mixed together and this was used to wash the pole. Yoghurt is thought to be a pure substance and is often used for cleansing ceremonies in the Sikh faith. While the pole was being washed, many of the worshippers came forward to touch the pole, and as they did so they bowed. When the pole had been dried, fresh strips of material were wrapped around it before it was put back in position with a new flag proudly flying from it. As it was erected,

109

Washing the flagpole

five men, representing the Panj Pyares referred to in the festival story, called out loudly, 'Jo bole so nihal', which means, 'the One who speaks is a blessed One'; the congregation responded, 'Sat sri akal', which means, 'God is truth'.

Once this ceremony was over, the Sikhs moved into the langar, the kitchen/dining area of the gurdwara, where a meal had been prepared. They ate their meal together in a spirit of great unity, for the ceremony they had just witnessed had reminded them of important aspects of their faith and their commitment to it.

Sunday

The gurdwara was full to overflowing when the worshippers assembled on Sunday. Since it was the celebration of Baisakhi there were more present than usual. It was a warm day for April and the large fans on the ceiling were switched on to help cool the air. Everything looked very colourful: the dress of the worshippers and the decorations in the gurdwara showed that this was a special day for the Sikh community.

Early that morning, the continuous reading from the Guru Granth Sahib had

110

been completed and since then the number of worshippers in the temple had steadily increased. Outside, many of them, as they reached the flagpole, bowed their heads in reverence before entering the building, where they immediately removed their shoes.

On this day there seemed to be activity in every room of the gurdwara: in the langar, the ladies were cooking chapatis and preparing a vegetable curry while one man was setting out tables ready for the communal meal. In another room four **ragis**, i.e. musicians, who had been specially invited to lead the music in the festival, were practising. Upstairs, the room used for worship which contained the holy book was full of people, and in the room adjoining it, preparations were being made for the Amrit ceremony in which several men and women were to take the serious step of committing themselves fully to the Sikh faith and way of life. Baisakhi is a popular time for this ceremony of commitment to take place since it was at Baisakhi that Guru Gobind first initiated the Khalsa.

This ceremony was to take place in private; only the Panj Pyares, the five men representing those five who were prepared to surrender their lives to Guru Gobind, were to be present together with the initiates. In the ceremony, the actions of the Guru when he baptised the first Khalsa members would be repeated and those who received Amrit would promise to live their lives according to the rules laid down by the Guru.

Preparing the meal

Worship on Baisakhi

We followed Mr and Mrs Athwall, two members of the Sikh community, into the room where the worship was to take place. We were grateful that they had volunteered to explain the various ceremonies for us. Each worshipper made a deep bow and presented an offering in front of the Guru Granth Sahib. Mrs Athwall later explained that some families had brought food as their offering and this would later be used in the langar, while others had given Romallas, which are ornate coverings for the holy book. They told us that people are especially generous with their offerings on this special day.

Sikhs regard it as a privilege to listen to the **gurbani**, the hymns of the Gurus,

The musicians

being chanted from the Guru Granth Sahib. Many of those present had been there all morning listening to these, but there was no sign of restlessness in this happy congregation.

The musicians whom we had noticed earlier were now seated on a stage to the right of the Guru Granth Sahib and they began to play, leading the hymn singing which is so important a part of Sikh worship. Mr Athwall explained that this is known as **kirtan**; one hymn followed another and all of them were in praise of God and the Gurus who had revealed God to men.

It is also a custom to listen to lectures at festival times; this is known as **katha** and it provides an opportunity for Sikhs to learn more about their faith. Three speakers addressed the congregation on this occasion; again, we were most grateful for the Athwall's help with translation! The Sikhs were reminded of the history of their faith and the speakers called for unity and brotherhood in the congregation, urging them to become 'saint soldiers' of the kind that Guru Gobind had created. Each of them ended by wishing the congregation 'a happy new year'.

In the Langar
At 1 p.m. everyone shared a communal meal in the langar; this consisted of chapatis, vegetable curry and rice. It was a very pleasant social occasion which provided an opportunity to greet friends and exchange news. The meal also demonstrated the unity and equality of the Sikhs. Mr Athwall told us that the people brought the food for the langar, but that on the occasion of this Baisakhi, so much had been given that a lorry had been loaded with surplus food and it had been delivered to a hospital nearby. Sikhs regard it as a duty to give, and the people had done so joyfully on this memorable day.

Ending the worship
In the afternoon, there were more songs to welcome the new year and, finally, everyone stood for the prayer known as the **Ardas**. As the prayer was being recited, one of the leaders in the congregation touched the mixture of Karah Parshad, which had been prepared, with a sword, which is said to symbolise strength. We all then received a portion of this sweet food in our cupped hands.

So Baisakhi worship came to an end and the congregation departed wishing each other 'a happy new year'. Before we left, we had the opportunity to speak to the president of the gurdwara about the celebrations we had witnessed. He told us: 'Our festivals are not meant only for rejoicing and fun. It is most important for us to remember that they provide an opportunity for us to rededicate ourselves to following the ideals of the Sikh faith. We must always remember the mission of the Gurus and aim to follow in their footsteps. By joining in these celebrations which involve hymn singing, sharing food in the langar, giving to charity and serving others, we celebrate in a way which is typical of our Sikh tradition.

'Baisakhi has always been an important time throughout Sikh history. On this date, Guru Amar Das ordered the Sikhs to assemble before him; on this date, Guru Gobind formed the Khalsa Panth, the 'pure men of God'. Before he died, the Guru said, "I have bestowed guruship to the Khalsa; Khalsa is my true self; I shall always live in the Khalsa." '

Task 1
Draw the emblem on the Sikh flag and explain its symbolic significance.

Task 2
The members of the Khalsa were ordered by Guru Gobind to wear five articles, each of which in Punjabi begins with the letter 'K'; these from now on would distinguish

Ardas

them as Sikhs and mark them out as men prepared to fight for the truth. The five 'Ks' are:

Kesh – long hair, a symbol of devotion to God.
Kara – a steel bracelet worn on the right wrist to remind a Sikh of his unity with God and the Khalsa.
Kanga – a comb: Sikhs must keep their long hair tidy and in place. This is a symbol of discipline.
Kirpan – a sword symbolising a willingness to fight for justice.
Kaachs – shorts worn to symbolise moral purity.

Sikhs who are committed to their faith still wear these five 'Ks' as symbols of their commitment. Why do you think the Guru insisted that the Sikhs should wear this uniform?

Task 3
What part is played by the following in Sikh worship: kirtan, katha, Karah Parshad?

Task 4
Guru Gobind said, 'It is righteous to take the sword.' Think of the situation when he formed the Khalsa and discuss whether you think he was right to do so. Do you agree with this statement which he made? Give reasons for your answer.

114

Divali

You read on page 29 about the importance to Hindus of the festival of Divali, the festival of light, which also marks the beginning of a new religious year for Hindus.

The Sikh new year occurs in April, but they too observe this popular festival of Divali in ways very similar to Hindus. In Sikh homes, divas are lit, presents are exchanged and children enjoy fireworks and bonfires.

These festivities are used by Sikhs, however, not to remember the victory of Rama and Sita over evil, as is the case with Hindus; Sikhs use the festival to celebrate an important event in Sikh history which actually happened at the time when Hindus were celebrating Divali.

The Festival Story

We learned on page 106 that Sikhism began in India and that, in fact, the founder of this faith, Guru Nanak, was born into a Hindu home. Many of the first Sikhs, or disciples of the Guru, were Hindus, so it was only natural that some Hindu celebrations continued to be a part of their lives. These festivals, however, took on a new and significant meaning for Sikhs as their religion developed. The victorious message of Divali, the triumph of goodness over evil, became most significant for them at the time of the sixth Guru of Sikhism, Guru Hargobind.

Guru Hargobind

In the days of the fifth Guru, Arjan, times were hard for Sikhs living in northern India. The Muslim emperor who ruled over India was called Jehangir; he arrested Arjan, who died while still the emperor's prisoner. Arjan's son, Hargobind, took over the leadership of the Sikhs in 1606. He established friendly relations with the emperor for a time since they both happened to be fond of hunting. It was not long, however, before Hargobind was suspected of treachery because he had gathered an army together and constructed a fort in the city of Amritsar which later was to become the famous centre of Sikhism. Hargobind's enemies told the emperor that the Guru was calling himself a king and was planning revenge for his father's death. As a result, Guru Hargobind was imprisoned in a fortress at Gwalior.

At this time there were fifty-two Hindu princes being held in the same prison. They were badly treated and given little food because they had conspired against the emperor. Hargobind gladly shared with them whatever food he was given. Sikhs used to come to the prison every day. They were not allowed to see their leader so they simply stood outside the prison walls and prayed. This protest went on day after day and, each day, there seemed to be more and more Sikhs standing silently outside the fortress. Eventually the emperor was told of this protest at the prison and he decided to investigate personally the charges against Hargobind. Finally he pronounced that the Guru was innocent and ordered his release: officers were sent to tell Hargobind that he could leave as a free man.

When the fifty-two princes heard the news, they were pleased for the Guru, but felt rather sorry for themselves for there was no suggestion that they would be released and they would now be denied the extra food, to supplement their poor diet, which Hargobind had passed on to them.

Hargobind reassured them, however, saying, 'I will not go and leave you here in this prison.' He turned to the emperor's officers and said, 'Tell the emperor that I thank him for his investigations but I will not leave here without my fifty-two friends. They must be released with me!'

The officers returned rather reluctantly to the emperor for they knew that such a message would not please him. The emperor was more puzzled than angry. He still wanted to release Hargobind to relieve the situation of unrest among the Sikhs, but he did not want to release the fifty-two rebel princes. Eventually he decided to give the Guru a problem which he felt sure Hargobind would not be able to solve. The officers were told to return to the prison and give the following message: 'The Guru must be released with honour but, as for the princes, they are dependent on Hargobind and so only as many as can pass through the doorway holding on to the Guru's clothing shall be allowed to leave!'

The emperor knew very well that the prison doorway was so narrow that not more than one person could pass through it at the same time!

The officers laughed as they returned to the prison, and said, 'These princes are starving, but they are not so thin that they can escape through that narrow exit!'

Guru Hargobind received the message calmly and sent his thanks to the emperor saying that he would leave the prison the next day. Since the emperor had suggested

Guru Hargobind

he could leave with honour, he asked for his cloak, which he wore on special occasions, to be sent to the prison.

The next day his cloak arrived. It was a long cloak with tassels all round the edges. The Guru told each prince to hold a tassel and said, 'Now, follow me to freedom!' One by one, the princes followed the Guru through the dark door of the prison into sunlight and freedom.

This event took place when Hindus were celebrating Divali and so Sikhs remember Guru Hargobind's victory for truth and freedom in their celebration of the festival.

The Celebrations

The children of the Sangha family returned home from school to find every room in their house illuminated with the little lamps known as **divas**; they were excited because they knew that their Divali festival had begun. Two days earlier, Akhand Path had begun in the gurdwara. Akhand Path is a continuous reading of the Guru Granth Sahib from beginning to end. It takes approximately forty-eight hours to complete and many who are trained to read the holy book give their services for two hours at a time. Mr Sangha had taken part in this reading which was completed on the day of Divali and many Sikhs had attended the gurdwara for some part of the reading. It was especially full as the reading came to an end; when the continuous reading was completed, all present received Karah Parshad, the Sikhs' holy food, made from flour, sugar, water and butter. All were also welcome to share in the meal which had been prepared in the langar, the kitchen which is a part of every gurdwara.

Questions about Divali

We asked the Sangha children what they particularly liked about Divali. One of them said, 'In Sikh homes, special sweets and other foods are prepared, friends and relatives visit us and we are given gifts.' Another of the children broke in to say, 'Oh yes, but I like when it is dark and the bonfire is lit and the fireworks are set off! These are things I especially like about Divali!'

We questioned Mr Sangha about the Sikh Divali customs.

Our question: Your children tell us that tonight you will have a bonfire and fireworks: can you tell us why these are part of your celebrations?

Answer: This custom goes back to the story behind our festival. When Guru Hargobind was released from the fortress at Gwalior, he travelled back to Amritsar. When he arrived he found that the temple was brightly lit with many divas and there was a display of fireworks to welcome him. That day was the Hindu festival of Divali and

such things have become part of our Sikh celebration.

Our question: What do you wish your children to remember especially about Divali?

Answer: I want them to remember, when they see the lights of the many divas, that goodness will conquer evil, just as the lights overcome the darkness. I also want them to grow up knowing the stories about our great leaders to whom we owe so much.

Our question: We have seen how excited your children are about this festival: can you describe for us your own feelings at this time?

Answer: I must confess that I still feel something of the thrill I used to experience as a child! Now, however, I think I feel especially proud to be a Sikh as I remember the struggles Sikhs have had in the past to keep the faith alive against much opposition. It gives me courage and reminds me that, as a member of the Khalsa, the brotherhood of Sikhs, I too must keep the faith and fight for truth and justice.

Our question: Do you attend the gurdwara for worship at Divali?

Answer: Oh yes! We have a special service today for it is most important for Sikhs to join together in worship. We listen to the words of the Gurus from our holy book, we meditate on God and thank him for our glorious leaders in the past who have shown us how to live our lives. We think too of the Golden Temple at Amritsar which today will be decorated with many divas. This place is very special to Sikhs; it would be a wonderful experience to go there to celebrate Divali; perhaps some day it may be possible!

Our question: Is this not really a Hindu festival which you are celebrating?

Answer: No! We do not regard it as a Hindu festival at all. One of the great Sikhs from our past said, 'Non-Sikh festivals should not be celebrated.' Even if we observe the

Distributing Karah Parshad

same day as Hindu Divali, we do it in our own way. Even before the time of Hargobind, whom we remember at Divali, Sikhs had been commanded by Guru Amar Das, the third of our Gurus, to appear before him at Divali. Instead of enjoying the Divali celebrations in the Hindu villages where they lived, they were being required to remember that they were Sikhs. By celebrating Divali as we do, we still consider that we are obeying the Guru's order to appear before him, for our Guru now is our holy book, the Guru Granth Sahib, and the holy book plays an important part in our celebration as it does in all our worship.

Task 1
Imagine you have to teach young children the story of Guru Hargobind. Draw a cartoon strip, following a sequence you think eight-year-olds would best understand.

Task 2
What can be learned from the story of Guru Hargobind which illustrates the way a true Sikh should live and behave?

Task 3
Mr Sangha told us that one of the great Sikhs from the past said, 'Non-Sikh festivals should not be celebrated.' Why do you think such an instruction was given? What do you think Sikhs would have missed if they had been unable to take such a non-Sikh festival and give it new meaning?

Task 4
Outline each of the various parts of the Sikh celebration of Divali and explain their religious significance.

118

Gurpurbs

There are a number of festivals observed by Sikhs which are known as Gurpurbs. These are anniversaries of special events such as the birth or the death of one of the Sikh Gurus. The word 'guru' means 'teacher' and altogether there were ten such leaders who brought God's message to the people of the Punjab in northern India between 1469 and 1708 CE. These men are especially honoured in Sikhism as historic and heroic figures – perfect men from whom Sikhs can learn of God.

Pictures of the Gurus can be seen in Sikh homes and in the gurdwara, the place of worship. The Gurus, however, are not worshipped by Sikhs; it is emphasised that these Gurus taught that there is one God and he alone is to be worshipped.

The word **Gurpurb** tells us that the anniversary being celebrated is a holy day; the syllable 'pur' actually means 'holiday'. The Sikhs, however, cannot take a holiday on every such occasion but they can remember the importance of these leaders by holding special celebrations. There are four Gurpurbs that Sikhs especially celebrate – the birthday of Guru Nanak, the martyrdoms of Guru Arjan and Guru Tegh Bahadur and the birthday of Guru Gobind – and we will look at the first three of these and the stories behind them. As far as the actual celebration is concerned, it is virtually the same for them all.

The Festival Stories

Guru Nanak's Birthday

Nanak was born in the village of Talwandi which, although now in Pakistan, was at the time in the Punjab, a fertile area of northern India. The two main religions in India at the time of his birth were Hinduism and Islam. Nanak was born into a Hindu family but northern India at the time was ruled by Muslims. Both these religions were to play a very significant part in developing Nanak's religious ideas.

Mehta Kalu, Nanak's father, had long wanted a son and he had great ambitions for the child's future. As is usual when a Hindu child is born, he called the priest to cast the boy's horoscope. The priest, Pandit Hadrial, asked for such information as the day and time of the birth and the mother's name; finally he declared that the child would guide many people and would achieve success.

Mehta Kalu was a business man and he hoped that the success foretold by the priest would come from Nanak's following in his footsteps. This, however, was not to be, for, although Nanak was a clever boy, he was not interested in the sort of work carried out by his father. Mehta Kalu discovered this when Nanak was still quite young. He tried to interest Nanak in business affairs by giving him twenty rupees and sending him to nearby towns to buy goods which could be sold in Talwandi at a profit.

Nanak took the money and set out with his friend, Bala. He was determined to please his father so the boys travelled from village to village searching for bargains. On reaching one town, however, they came across a group of holy men who were starving. Nanak stopped to talk to them and they explained that the crops had failed and the people had nothing left over to give to them. Sandhus, or holy men, give up all their possessions and devote their lives entirely to God, depending on others for food. Nanak, on hearing of their plight, gave the twenty rupees to the holy men, saying that this was the best way to use the money.

Nanak's friend, Bala, was horrified at such an action for he knew that Nanak's father would be angry. Bala's fears were justified for on their arrival home Nanak was soundly beaten by his father who remained unconvinced by Nanak's explanation that human life was more important than money.

Despite this lack of interest in making money, Nanak took a job as a modi, or storekeeper, for the Muslim governor of Sultanpur. Local landowners had to give part of their crops to the governor as a form of tax and it was Nanak's job to check their contributions. He worked in this position for twelve years and during this time he married and became the father of two sons.

As a young boy he was greatly interested in religion and his love of God grew in his adult life. Every morning he rose early, bathed in the river and offered prayers; he followed the same practice in the evening; often others joined him and they sang hymns to God well into the night.

Nanak at Thirty Years Old

When he was thirty years old, Nanak had an experience which completely changed his way of life. After his early morning

bathe in the river, Nanak disappeared. For three days no one knew where he was and some feared that he had drowned. On his return he remained completely silent for a day and then proclaimed the truth that he had learned in his absence: 'There is neither Hindu nor Muslim...God is neither Hindu nor Muslim and the path which I follow is God's.' Nanak had discovered this truth in a vision which he described as 'being taken to the court of God'. He felt himself called by God to go and preach to the people and remind them about God.

Nanak left his wife and children and set out on a series of journeys which were to take him to many places in India. He was accompanied on his travels by a Muslim follower called Mardana. In every place they visited, he told the people to love God, love their fellow men and work hard for their living. Often he put his teaching into the form of hymns and, accompanied by Mardana, he sang the great truths he wished to convey.

During his travels, Nanak, who was now given the title 'guru' by his followers, spoke out against the social evils which he saw. The caste system, which was so much a part of Hinduism, divided people and was deplored by the Guru; he also disliked the low status given to women. He attacked the religious rituals which people practised sometimes only because they were superstitious. He visited the great centres of religion and, by his actions, tried to open people's minds to certain truths. Once, when he visited Mecca, the holy city of the Muslims, he slept with his feet pointing in the direction of the Kaaba, that most sacred building in Mecca. The people complained that he was being disrespectful but Nanak simply replied, 'Take my feet and point them where God is not!'

He also visited Hardwara, a place of Hindu pilgrimage, and joined the pilgrims in the River Ganges. Many people were in the river, praying for their ancestors and throwing water eastwards to the rising

Guru Nanak

sun. Nanak turned to the west and threw water in that direction. The pilgrims wondered at this strange action but Nanak said, 'If you can throw water for your ancestors, I can throw water for my farm in the Punjab!' In these and many other ways, Nanak tried to remind people to be simple and sincere in their worship; a person's motives were more important than deeds done to impress others.

Kartapur

When the Guru was fifty years old, he settled in a place called Kartapur; his family joined him, as did other disciples and a religious community grew up there. The Guru built a place for worship in which daily acts of worship were performed; later, Sikhs were to call such a building a 'gurdwara', a word which means, 'the door of the guru'. The people were self-sufficient, worked hard and gave food to those in need in a free kitchen which had become part of their place of worship. The Guru told his followers, who became known as Sikhs, that they should meditate on the name of God and should sing the hymns which he had composed which contained much of his teaching.

A Successor Chosen

Before he died, Nanak chose a successor to lead the Sikhs. This man was Lehna, but the Guru renamed him Angad, which means, 'my limb' or 'part of me'. To his community of followers, the Guru handed on the hymns he had composed which later were to be included in the book which became the Sikh's holy book, the Guru Granth Sahib.

Guru Nanak left a community devoted to meditation on the name of God, honest living and sharing with others. He had, in fact, started a movement which was to grow and flourish under a succession of nine other famous teachers.

Martyrdom of Guru Arjan

Arjan became the fifth Guru of the Sikhs in 1581 CE. During his period of leadership Sikhism grew, for Arjan was a great organiser and an able administrator. He decided that the Sikhs needed a gurdwara in their city of Amritsar and he ordered the building of the Golden Temple in 1589. When it was completed, the hymns of the Gurus as well as those of Hindu and Muslim teachers were collected and, on Arjan's instructions, placed in the Temple. These writings were called the **Adi Granth**, which means 'the first collection'; this became the basis of the holy book of the Sikhs which was to become known as the Guru Granth Sahib which means, 'Lord Teacher Book'.

One reason for the expansion of the Sikh faith at this time was the rule of a wise and tolerant emperor. This Muslim emperor was called Akbar and he was known to treat his subjects fairly and with justice. Akbar was a devout Muslim but was willing to respect the beliefs of others and he allowed Sikhs and Hindus living under his jurisdiction in northern India to practise their own religions.

Some people tried to create trouble by saying that Guru Arjan had ordered a book to be written which contained teachings

122

against the emperor's faith. In fact, when the emperor examined the Adi Granth, he was so pleased with its contents that he gave a gift of gold to the book and other gifts to those who had brought it to him.

When Akbar died in 1605 he was succeeded by his son, Jehangir, a man with very different views about religion. His reign began in turmoil, for his own son, Khusrau, was known to be the favourite grandson of Akbar. Many said that Akbar had wished Khusrau to rule after him and they encouraged him to rebel against his father. Six months after Jehangir became emperor, Khusrau raised an army and fought against his father. Jehangir showed no mercy and soon overcame his son and his rebel army, chasing them as they withdrew through the country. He finally caught up with them and put all the rebels to death.

Jehangir was to be equally merciless with anyone he suspected of giving aid to his son. He was very suspicious of the growing popularity of the Sikh faith and the respect shown to its leader, Guru Arjan. When a report reached him that Arjan had assisted the rebel prince and had even given shelter to him, he willingly ordered his arrest.

Arjan denied the charge of treason and refused to pay the fine imposed on him as a punishment. He was, therefore, taken to Lahore and condemned to death by torture. This torture lasted three days and on the third, the Guru was drowned in the River Ravi. On 30th May 1606 his body was carried away by the strong currents and was never recovered.

Guru Arjan was, therefore, the first martyr of the Sikh faith. His great example of loyalty to the truth was to be an inspiration to those who were to face persecution in future years, for hard times were ahead for the Sikhs in the Punjab. Arjan had preached 'enmity with none and friendship for all' and his death showed his great courage and patience. His words live on in the hymns sung in gurdwaras and his memory remains in the minds of Sikhs who celebrate his victory for truth.

Martyrdom of Guru Tegh Bahadur

Tegh Bahadur, the ninth Guru, was the grandson of Arjan, and his grandfather's noble sacrifice no doubt made a great impression on him. Seven years before it was necessary to choose the ninth Guru of the Sikhs, the rule of a new emperor named Aurangzeb began. When Tegh Bahadur was proposed as the ninth Guru, the emperor opposed this choice and so did other rivals within Sikhism. Tegh Bahadur, however, proved to have the essential qualities for the difficult age in which the Sikhs were living. He spent his early years as Guru preaching in areas outside the Punjab, spreading the message of the faith.

As the years of Aurangzeb's rule progressed, the emperor became increasingly intolerant: he wished everyone to follow his religion of Islam. He began a campaign to force people to become Muslims; Hindu temples and schools were closed and mosques were built in their place. Sikhs were treated harshly and everyone who would not accept Islam was heavily taxed.

The situation grew increasingly hopeless for those who wanted to follow their own faith and it was clear that they needed a leader who would guide them in such a difficult time. Tegh Bahadur proved to be such a leader; he travelled around north-west India urging people, both Sikhs and Hindus, to remain loyal to their faiths. Crowds listened to him and were strengthened by the Guru's words.

Aurangzeb finally ordered the Guru's arrest; he was taken to Delhi and kept in captivity while attempts were made to convert him to Islam. If this had been successful, then almost certainly all the opposition to the emperor's policy would have vanished. Tegh Bahadur's three closest companions had also been arrested and were with him in Delhi; one by one they were tortured in front of him and each died bravely, refusing to give in to Aurangzeb's demands, and keeping their eyes firmly fixed on the Guru.

The Guru Beheaded

On 11th November 1675, it was the Guru's turn to face martyrdom. This brave leader of the Sikhs, after saying his prayers, made a deep bow and, as he had requested, was beheaded. His body was taken out into the streets of Delhi and displayed as a warning to others who resisted the emperor. Some daring Sikhs captured the body of their leader and cremated it according to Sikh custom.

The Guru's death became an inspiration to Sikhs and Hindus alike who lived in northern India; he had chosen to make a stand for religious freedom and to display his belief, publicly, in the principles of the Sikh faith.

The Celebrations

Akhand Path

All the Gurpurbs are celebrated in a similar fashion and all begin with the Akhand Path, the continuous reading from the holy book described on page 117.

Since it takes forty-eight hours to read the whole of the Guru Granth Sahib, Akhand Path begins two days before the actual celebration of the Gurpurb. As we have already seen in other Sikh festivals, many Sikhs attend to witness the beginning of the reading.

The prayer known as **Anand Sahib** is recited at the beginning of the worship; it opens with the words:

'I have reached God, the Supreme Spirit, and all my sorrows have vanished. My sorrows, afflictions and sufferings have departed by hearing the true word. The saints and holy men are glad on hearing it from the perfect Guru.'

When this prayer, composed by the third Guru, Amar Das, is completed, everyone stands with hands clasped together, facing the Granth, to say the Ardas, the central prayer of Sikhism. (See our book, *Believers*, pages 94-5.)

After Ardas, the Granthi, the person who is first to read a portion of the holy book, turns its pages at random and reads a few verses to the congregation; such random selection from the book is known as **hukam** and shows the importance which Sikhs place on the book as a source of guidance. A Kirpan (sword) is placed on the Karah Parshad, and everyone receives a small portion of the food which symbolises equality and brotherhood.

The continuous reading then begins. During the course of the reading, many Sikhs come at intervals to sit and listen and then quietly depart when it is time for work or other duties.

The Day of the Gurpurb
The reading finishes early on the morning of the Gurpurb. Often this is Sunday since it is a day when the maximum number of people can attend. Usually the gurdwara is full of men, women and children for this conclusion of the reading. It is followed by the normal act of worship with hymns and, on Gurpurbs, speakers who discuss the importance of the Gurus in the Sikh faith. Since these are special occasions, visiting musicians are often invited to play and sing in the worship which continues all morning.

Both men and women are busy in the langar on the occasion of Gurpurbs. The women make chapatis, rice dishes, vegetable curries and special sweet foods. It is considered a privilege to help others and many volunteer to serve, especially the men. A free meal is distributed every Sunday in this particular gurdwara to any who wish to attend, but on Gurpurbs, extra numbers must be catered for.

In the worship, after Ardas and the receiving of Karah Parshad, the people eat their meal in a festive mood and celebrations may well continue all day!

In the langar

Procession with the Granth

In India, on the occasion of Gurpurbs, the Granth is carried with great honour through the streets. This is not always possible in Britain, but sometimes special arrangements are made for it to be done. In the photograph on this page you can see one such occasion. The Sikhs were celebrating the Birthday of Guru Gobind and they hired a lorry which they decorated with flowers; the Granth was placed on the lorry and a canopy erected over it. The lorry was driven slowly through the streets and a procession of Sikhs followed, publicly honouring their tenth Guru and the book which is all-important to them.

Questions about Gurpurbs

We asked Mr Singh, who regularly serves in the langar in the gurdwara in our community, about Gurpurbs.

Our question: What do you see as the importance of celebrating the Gurpurbs?

Answer: To me, of course, they are annual celebrations of great significance. I remember the Gurpurbs in India and I am very proud when I see the whole community coming together here in Britain to honour the Gurus. It is important also for the young ones to hear the teachings and stories of the Gurus. You have seen the fellowship that the people have here in the gurdwara; the Gurus unite us as we think of the traditions passed down to us from them. We, as Sikhs, have fought to keep our faith and to be true to the teachings of the Gurus through long years of our history. When we hear the stories from the past, we are proud to be Sikhs and it gives an opportunity to resolve again to be the kind of people who are worthy of the example given by the Gurus.

Task 1
Design a poster to remind Sikhs in the community that it is Guru Nanak's birthday. Make sure that you include such details as the time Akhand Path is to begin and when it is to finish. Give details of other items which may be important in the celebration. (It takes place in November.)

Task 2
Write the conversation between Guru Nanak and his father when *either*
  (a) he returned home after giving the twenty rupees to the holy men, *or*
  (b) he decided to leave his family and follow God's call to preach.

Task 3
What features of the Gurpurb emphasise equality and brotherhood? In what ways are these supportive of the Gurus' own ideas of the correct way to live?

Task 4
'Persecution often defeats its own ends.' Write an essay in support of this statement using the stories of Arjan and Tegh Bahadur to assist you.

General Tasks

1 'There is something in man which makes him want to celebrate!' Discuss this statement, trying to express why you think celebrations are so important.

Which of the religious festivals you have studied have events lying behind them which you consider are worth celebrating and which, in your opinion, are less worthy of celebration? Give reasons for your answer.

2 'Religious Education is essentially about meaning, purpose and values.' In what way has your study of festivals helped you to think about the meaning and purpose of life and about what is particularly valuable in life?

3 What similarities can you see in the festivals you have studied, even though they are in different religious faiths? Illustrate your answer by referring to specific festivals and to the features which they have in common.

Why do you think there are such common elements?

4 Which of the festivals you studied involved a procession of witness? Why do you think this was an important aspect of the celebration in these particular faiths?

5 Which festivals involve some sort of sacrifice on the part of those who are celebrating? Why are such festivals involving sacrifice still occasions of great joy?

6 Divali, Chanukah and Easter are sometimes known as 'festivals of light'; why do you think light is such an important religious symbol and why does it feature especially in these festivals?

7 Often at festival times people remember great acts of deliverance. Choose two festivals which remind the worshippers of such acts in their history; describe the act remembered and try to explain why it is still of great importance today.

8 Festivals are often occasions when people express fellowship and love; choose four festivals and explain how in the celebrations people show their care and concern for others.

9 Which festivals do you think provide the worshippers with an opportunity to show, openly, commitment to their beliefs? Describe how the people do this, stating clearly the beliefs which are being expressed.

10 Special foods play a part in many festivals. Choose three festivals described in this book and explain what food is especially significant in the celebration. Why do you think food is an important part of such celebrations?

11 Why do you think all festivals are celebrated annually? What marks a religious celebration out as being different from a secular one, e.g. a birthday?

12 Some festivals have extra significance because they are celebrated at a particular time or season of the year. Which festivals would you place in this category? Give reasons for your answer.

13 Festivals are communal gatherings; what value do you see in a body of people gathering together to celebrate? Would the celebration of a festival be as effective if the individual observed it alone? Give reasons for your answer.

14 Choose four festivals and design a symbol for each one which you think best expresses the meaning of it.

Index

Abraham 36, 45, 102
Adhan 99
Adi Granth 122-3
Afikoman 60, 61
Agni 29
Akhand Path 108, 117, 124-5
Amar Das 107, 113, 118, 125
Amrit 107
Amritsar 115, 117, 122
Anand Sahib 124-5
Angad 122
Antiochus Epiphanes 50, 53, 54
Apocrypha 51, 53
Ardas 113
Arjan 115, 119, 122-4
Ark 47
Arti 10-11, 16, 20, 31
Atonement, Day of (Yom Kippur) 35, 38-42
Aum 7
Avatars 7, 12

Bar Mitzvah 48
Bhagavad-Gita 14, 33
Bhajans 9, 19
Bharata 9, 24, 28, 29
Bimah 48
Brahma, 8, 12, 22

Chag Haurim (Chanukah) 50-4
Chakra 109
Chametz 56
Charoset 58
Christingle 67-8, 70
Coconuts 21, 22
Communion 68-70, 79

Days of Awe 35
Deuteronomy, Book of 47
Dhan Trausti 30-1
Divas, 10, 31-2, 33, 116, 117
Dreidel 52-3, 54
Du'a 92
Durga 23, 24-8
Durga Puja (Navaratri and Dussera) 23-8

Easter Vigil 75-9
Elijah 59
Etrog 45-6
Exodus, Book of 59, 61

Fasting 40, 41, 91-2, 94-5, 96-7

Garba 26-7, 28
Genesis, Book of 47, 55
Geshem 46
Ghee 32
Gloria 79
Gobind 107, 109, 111, 113, 119, 126
Good Friday 74-5, 79, 80
Gopis 22

Granthi 125
Gregorian calendar 63
Gurbani 112-13
Guru Granth Sahib 108, 110-11, 112-13, 117, 118, 122, 124, 125, 126

Haggadah 57, 60
Hajj 101-3, 105
Hallah bread 37, 44
Hallel 46
Hanuman 24, 25, 28
Hargobind 115-16, 117
Hatan Berayshis 48
Hatan Torah 48
Hiranyakashup 17
Holika 17-18, 22
Holocaust 60
Holy Spirit 82-3
Holy Week 71-5
Hoshanah Rabbah 46
Hukam 125

Iftar 92
Ihtekaf 92
Isaac 36, 45, 102
Isaiah, Book of 41
Ishmael 102

Jacob 37, 45
Janamashtami (Lord Krishna's birthday) 12-16
Jonah, Book of 41
Judas Maccabaeus 50-1, 52, 53
Judith, Book of 53

Kaaba 85-6, 87, 94, 99
Kansa 12-14, 18, 22
Karah Parshad 108, 117, 125
Karpas 58
Katha 113
Khalsa 107-8, 109, 111, 113
Khanda 108-9
Kirtan 113
Kol Nidre 40
Krishna 12-16, 18-19, 22, 30
Ks, the five 113-14

Lailat ul-Qadr 94
Lakshmana 9, 24, 28, 29
Lakshmi 30-2
Langar 110, 111, 112, 113
Latkes 53
Leviticus, Book of 35, 41, 45
Lotus Flower 31
Lulav 45-6

Maccabees 53, 54
Mattathias 50, 52, 53
Matzoth (Matzah) 56, 60, 61
Maundy Thursday 73-4
Mawlid ul-Nabi (the Birthday of the Prophet) 85-8

Menorah 51-2
Mina 101, 102
Moror 58, 61
Moses 35, 43, 45, 55-6, 58

Nanak 106, 115, 119-22
Neilah 41-2
Nishan Sahib 108-10, 111
Numbers, Book of 41

Om 7

Palm Sunday 72-3
Panj Pyares 107, 110, 111
Pentecost (Shavuot) 43, 81 (Whitsun) 81-3
Pesach (Passover) 43, 55-62
Pilgrimage see Hajj
Pilgrim Festivals 43
Prahlad 17-18
Prashad 11, 20, 21, 27, 31, 33
Prayer call 99
Puja 31
Puranas 7
Putana 18, 22

Qur'an 90-1, 92, 94, 97, 98, 102

Radha 18, 19, 30
Ragis 111
Rakat 92
Rama 8-11, 23-5, 27-8, 29-30, 33
Ramayana 8, 9
Ravana 8, 9, 24, 29
Romallas 112

Sanatan dharma 7
Scapegoat 39
Seder 56-62
Shammash 51-2
Shema 42
Shiva 12, 22
Shofar 36, 42
Sita 23-5, 27-8, 29-30, 33
Suhoor 92
Sukkah 43-5

Tallith 49
Tashlich 37-8
Tegh Bahadur 119, 124
Temple (Jerusalem) 38-9, 41, 50-1, 53, 54, 58
Torah 35, 36, 43, 46-8
Tzedakah 41

Vasudeva 12-14
Vedas 9
Vishnu 8, 12, 13, 22, 30

Yahrzeit 40
Yathrib 98-9
Yizkor 41